Happy Days
John

from

Dad

PARTY BOOK

Distributed by
E. P. DUTTON & CO., INC.
300 Fourth Ave., New York 10, N. Y.

FOR FUN LOVING PEOPLE

When Kelvinator, oldest maker of electric refrigeration for the home, developed and produced the first Foodarama, a new, high mark in gracious living was reached. To quote a well-satisfied user—*"Foodarama living is better living for everyone,* and it is marked by four important characteristics: Foodarama families eat better . . . save money . . . save time . . . and have more fun, too!"— These are the things thousands of users have told us about Food-arama, the world's only combination of 6-cubic foot, upright home freezer and 12-cubic foot, self-defrosting refrigerator — both contained in a single compact cabinet.

Preparation of this complete Foodarama Party Book was inspired by users' comments such as this: "Foodarama families do more entertaining because it is so much easier. Everything is prepared in advance so you have more time to spend with your guests. There's plenty of space to store teen-age treats and Dad's favorite beverages. With Foodarama in the kitchen, Mother has more time for joining in the family fun."

This Foodarama Party Book is dedicated, therefore, to the thousands of people who already are enjoying Foodarama, and to the thousands more who soon will be using this completely new kind of modern foodkeeper.

This book of parties for every kind of holiday and occasion has been prepared and published in the hope that it will be helpful to all homemakers, everywhere, who are looking for new ideas in party giving—new foods to serve, new ways of doing things, new decorations to use, new games to play.

May all your parties be happy ones!

Joan Adams

Director, Kelvinator Institute
for Better Living

CONTENTS

3

4

HOW TO PLAN YOUR PARTY

It has often been said, by the wisest of hostesses, that the most important ingredients in any party are pencil and paper! A party doesn't just happen—it can't be "whipped up" from a package mix, or bought, "assorted," at the variety store. A successful party should be planned, well in advance, and down to the last detail. So get your pencil and paper and, using the outline below as a guide, let's plan your party!

THEME

What kind of occasion will it be? A party theme gives zestfulness to any occasion, piquancy to any setting. And a specific theme simplifies planning, for it gives a focal point for all the party elements. Holidays—Christmas, Easter, Thanksgiving, Hallowe'en, etc.—have simple, colorful, built-in themes. But why limit party-time to holidays? Endless opportunities exist for festive affairs: Showers, Anniversaries, Bridge Parties; Luncheons or Barbecues to welcome neighborhood newcomers; Tea Parties, Big and Little, to honor the visiting firemen and to reunite all those sorority sisters one hasn't seen in just too long a time! Themes for these varied occasions may be keyed to the seasons, or to the purpose of the gathering, or even to a favorite hobby or avocation of the person for whom the celebration is being given. Some imaginative hostesses prefer to build an entire theme around one special recipe (has it an international or regional character?)—or a prized possession which may set the keynote as a centerpiece—or even attractive, unusual china or serving accessories. Once *your* theme is set, proceed to . . .

GUEST LIST

Determine the size of your guest list by such considerations as: space, the kind of service you plan—buffet, dinner, cake and

coffee, etc., and whether you wish this to be an intimate gathering to entertain The Boss and Wife, or a big, informal party for old and dear friends.

INVITATIONS

Telephone or written invitations should be made or sent at least 10 days in advance of the party. (In the holiday seasons, issue invitations two to three weeks in advance—other hostesses also like to give holiday affairs!) An "RSVP" on a written invitation, or an "RSVP" call a day or two before the party will serve as a reminder to your guests, and as a final guest-list check for you. Charming invitations, in keeping with your party theme, may be purchased inexpensively at your stationer's. Or, better yet, make them yourself! For example: you plan a birthday party and the date falls very close to Easter, which you make your theme. A simple, attractive invitation may be made in this way: draw an egg shape on a piece of scrap paper. Make it a size to fit a standard-sized envelope. Cut out this outline drawing and use as a pattern. Fold a sheet of colored construction paper in half, and lay your pattern on it, with one side touching the fold of the paper. Hold in place, and trace around the pattern. Now cut out your design, being careful not to cut along the *entire* fold side, for this gives you a double paper, joined together at the one side. Now, decorate the front cover of the "egg." Use bands of colored tape or paper (glued-on), glitter or sequins, seals, paint or crayon designs, etc. Write your party data on the inside of the invitation in ink or crayon.

Always include all data in the invitation: Date and time (and unless you're prepared to watch the sunrise with at least one insomniac guest, give an "ending" time for the party, too!); the kind of occasion and the purpose (a birthday dinner for John, a Valentine Party just for fun, a tea in Cousin Agatha's honor); the place (be sure to give address and directions for first-time guests coming to your home).

MENU

Decide what your menu will be, and also the quantities you will need for the number of guests you plan to invite. Consider, with your theme and menu in mind, what table service and accessories you will use. (See Page 9 for tips on table settings.)

DECORATIONS

Balloons, crepe paper streamers, paper ribbons, fresh flowers and leaves are party standards. But here is the point at which your imagination really takes over! Party props are great fun to use, and add immeasurably to party atmosphere. Flags, pictures, pennants, antiques, hobby and sports equipment, models, even your children's toys may be used to create a gay, imaginative setting.

ENTERTAINMENT

Unlike the formal occasions of yesteryear, today's informal gatherings don't make guests a captive audience to the dubious entertainments of lady soloists or string quartets. Today's guests like to do-it-themselves, via games and quizzes, community singing, square and social dancing. The wise hostess is always prepared with a plan for a few games or activities, game props and prizes. Some occasions take naturally to games, others blossom with just an ice-breaker activity and/or after-dinner quizzes at the table. And some parties are so dominated by a steady stream of good conversation that games could be intrusions on the guests' self-created fun. Be prepared with a few games, just in case—or just for fun, and adapt any of the old favorites to your party theme by changing game name and props to fit. (See Party Games, Page 12, for game ideas.) Prizes are optional, but if they are used, they need be no more than tokens, and should be prettily-wrapped.

* * *

From your party plan, make a master shopping list—for supermarket, stationer's, florist, etc. Once your invitations are out, your party is underway; no more need be done but to work your plan.

* * *

This same planning approach applies to parties for youngsters of all ages. But there are a few age-group differences that the hostess will want to take into consideration in her planning.

PARTIES FOR CHILDREN

AGE TWO AND UNDER If you can't resist celebrating your little angel's arrival, then don't fool yourself. Leave him alone, invite adults who may in some small measure understand your sense of accomplishment, and celebrate with them, highlighting the party with a two-minute appearance of the star.

PRE-SCHOOLERS These parties should be short and simple. An hour to an hour and a half is long enough to celebrate. Cookies or cake and milk. Simple entertainment—a brief story, a nursery school type of game or two (emphasis on group activities—no competitive games) and simple, but colorful decorations: balloons, plastic cups from the table are take-home favors, party baskets with not too many candies in them, paper bags to take home the loot.

FIVE TO EIGHT YEAR OLDS Plenty of party atmosphere, great enthusiasm for costume parties, much concentration on Ice Cream and Cake (although eyes are bigger than capacities). Games should let the contestants MOVE, but the experienced hostess will alternate active games with quiet ones.

NINE TO ELEVEN Now interested in helping to plan the party and in making decorations, invitations and favors. Very appreciative of party atmosphere, but even more appreciative of food. Can consume unbelievable quantities of everything edible! Often prefer all-boy or all-girl parties, and enjoy all kinds of games, both active and quiet. Need room to move or the walls will!

JUNIOR AND SENIOR TEENS Teens can take the initiative in party planning, but need adult cooperation. Even more appreciative by now of clever decorations and table settings, also highly aware of party fare which must be attractive and ample. Senior Teens may prefer concentration on record spinning and dancing, but few groups can sustain an entire party session of this. Pencil and paper games, and active games are most enjoyed.

The parties in this book are offered as suggestions to give you ideas from which to take off on your own. If you view each occasion as a new adventure, and hold onto that wonderful sense of fun which made you want to "give a party" in the first place, you can't go wrong!

TABLE SETTINGS
and TABLE DECORATIONS

Decorative casseroles and chafing dishes, handsome electrical appliances, attractive, colorful table accessories—all these serving aids not only simplify your entertaining, they can enhance your table settings. Sparkling glass, silver and dishes, lovely linen and table decorations share equally in making your table a reflection of your hospitality.

INFORMAL DINNER

Use an attractive cloth (over table pad) or place mats. At each setting, place bottom edge of dinner plate and silverware an inch in from the table edge. (See the diagram below, but use only the silverware required for your specific menu.) The napkin fold is to the left. The first course may be served in the living room. Or, just before the guests come to the table, place the first course and salad on the table, fill water glasses, put a butter pat onto each bread and butter plate (these plates are optional). Dessert and coffee may be served with their necessary silverware.

INFORMAL DINNER

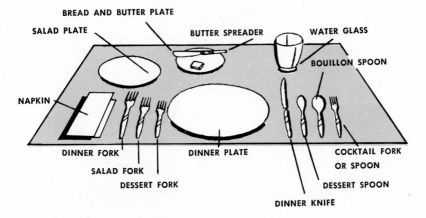

BREAD AND BUTTER PLATE

SALAD PLATE   BUTTER SPREADER   WATER GLASS

BOUILLON SPOON

NAPKIN

DINNER FORK   DINNER PLATE   COCKTAIL FORK OR SPOON

SALAD FORK

DESSERT FORK   DESSERT SPOON

DINNER KNIFE

LUNCHEON

The luncheon setting closely approximates the informal dinner setting. (See the diagram below, but limit your silverware set-ups to your own menu requirements.) The first course may be served in the living room or at the table. Dessert and coffee may be served similarly, and with their necessary silverware.

LUNCHEON

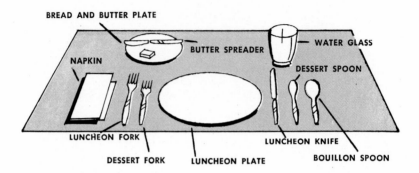

BUFFET

Use a pretty cloth (over a table pad) to suit the occasion. Buffet menus stress "fork" foods (include no foods difficult to cut). Rolls and breads are pre-buttered. If the table is placed against one wall, arrange foods and service so guests can move easily and freely around the open sides. One convenient arrangement for your food dishes, plates, etc., is this: napkins, dinner plates, hot and cold dishes, salad, bread, relishes, forks (see diagram below). If the table is placed out from the wall, spread out the setting to encompass all four sides. For large crowds you may use duplicate service; draw an imaginary line diagonally across the table, and set out two identical and complete services, one on either side of the "line." Coffee and dessert may be served from a side table, or you may prefer to serve these up in the kitchen and bring them into the living room.

BUFFET TABLE

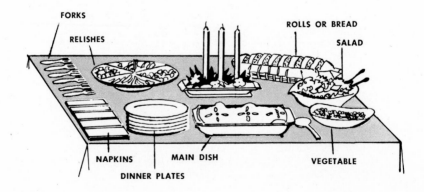

TEA PARTY

At the large tea, both tea and coffee are served. An attractive cloth, or runner and/or mats, cover a large dining or living room table. At one end of the table, place the tea tray which holds: pot of hot tea, pot of hot water, creamer, bowl of lump sugar with tongs, plate of lemon slices with fork. Cups and saucers, with spoons in place, are at back and sides of tray (the spoon is placed on the saucer at the back of the cup, with its handle parallel to the cup handle). Place your coffee service tray at the opposite end of the table. A friend of the hostess is asked to preside as "pourer" at each tray. Dessert plates, napkins and tea snacks are arranged attractively in between the trays (see diagram below). Serve only "finger" foods—nothing messy or sticky, and replenish food plates often.

TEA PARTY TABLE

COFFEE SERVICE

TEA SERVICE

PETITS FOURS

TEA SANDWICHES

TABLE DECORATIONS

Color helps to create mood. Cloth, napkins and china may be of contrasting colors, designs or textures, but the overall scheme should be harmonious and pleasing to the eye. When guests are seated at the table, use low centerpieces, perhaps baskets or low bowls of flowers or greens, or small ceramic figures combined with a few flowers on a mirror base. Candles, to the contrary, must be tall enough for the flame to be above eye-level of the guests when seated, and if candles are a part of table decor, they should be lighted. (Candles are never used at a luncheon table unless the room is dark.) For buffet and tea tables, tall candles and center-pieces create a more balanced setting (see Buffet Party, Page 56, and Tea Parties, Page 30, for decorating tips).

PARTY

GAMES

MAD MASKS On a work-table, lay out these materials: grocery bags large enough to fit over the head; construction paper, cellophane, crepe paper; bits of feathers, veiling, ribbons; cotton batting or yarn for "beards"; sequins and glitter, colored straws and toothpicks; scissors, paste, pins; crayons or watercolors. Marvelously decorated "masks" (cut holes in bags for eyes) can be made from the grocery bags, using any or all of the design materials. Judge the finished products for "Most Beautiful, Most Awful, Most Unbelievable," and award token prizes.

ELOPEMENT Teams of couples compete against each other, or couple against couple compete on a time basis. Starting from one side of the party room, each couple picks up a suitcase which contains two old-fashioned, loose-fitting nightgowns and nightcaps. They rush across the room, set down the suitcase, take out the nightclothes and put them on (over their street clothes), run back to the starting line, remove the nightclothes, replace them and close the suitcase, and hand it to the next couple who repeats the same action, and so on.

ALL TIME FAVORITES TREASURE HUNT: Hide candies such as jelly beans and Christmas candies, Easter eggs, etc. or hide paper cut-outs of pumpkins, turkeys, valentines, redeemed after the Hunt for candies, token prizes or a dance with the prettiest girl. OBSERVATIONS: Lay 25 objects on a table, and give contestants 3 to 5 minutes to study them. Contestants then leave the room and write down the objects. The player with most correct items listed wins. PIN THE TAIL: On the donkey, the bunny or black cat.

GAMES OF SKILL APPLE DART: Each player throws 3 darts at apples floating in a pan and scores 5 points per apple hit. RING TOSS: Drive 9 large nails, 3 to 4 inches apart, into a board; give each a point value (5, 10, etc.) which is marked in crayon under the nail; each contestant, standing well back from the board, tosses 3 small hoops over the nails. WALK THE TIGHTROPE: Lay an 8-foot string in a straight line on the floor. Contestants "walk the tightrope" while looking at the string through a pair of binoculars.

CIRCLE GAMES HOT POTATO: Players stand in a ring and pass a potato around the ring in time to music. When the music stops, the player holding the potato is out of the game. NUMBER TAG: Players sit in a circle and number off. A caller stands in the circle center. He suddenly calls out two numbers, and the players with those numbers must try to exchange seats without being tagged by the caller. If tagged, player becomes caller.

RACES These may be held outdoors, or in a party room cleared for action. Mark start and finish lines, or use opposite walls as the boundaries. PAPER BAG RACE: Contestants wear a grocery bag on each foot. BRONCO RACE: Contestants race on all fours (hands and feet). ANKLE DIZZY: Each contestant grabs his ankles with his hands, turns around three times, straightens up and races, if he's able, to the finish line. THREE-LEGGED RACE: Contestants race in pairs, side by side, with arms linked, and with their two inside legs tied together. SIDEWAYS SIDLE: Teams line up Indian file, each player locks his arms around the waist of the team-mate in front of him, and the team jumps sideways over the finish line.

BIRTHDAY PARTIES

Probably the most beloved of all parties is the Birthday Party, and why not? What more expressive way to show your affection for spouse, offspring, Uncle Johannes or Madame Chairman of the club's Used Clothing Drive than to celebrate his or her birth date with a party!

Use those traditional birthday decorations — overhead paper streamers, balloons, Japanese lanterns, etc. But for your very next birthday celebration, try keying your color scheme to the lovely, delicate colors of the "Four Tier Birthday Cake" (on the cover). For a charming table, use a pastel or white cloth, a flower-bowl centerpiece with flowers matching one or more of the cake's pastel colors; tall, white candles flank the centerpiece, each candle-holder base encircled by a tiny garland of the centerpiece flowers. Circles, cut from matching construction paper, repeat the cake motif, and are scattered over the table surface as well as pasted to the table-cloth edges to form a colorful border.

The handsome "Real Crazy" Cake, for 14-year-old partygoers (Page 18), serves as a perfect kick-off for a "Real Crazy" or "Mixed-up" Birthday Party. The birthday-host greets each guest with a warm-hearted "Happy Birthday" greeting, and a token "Birthday" present to unwrap. Decorations from Christmas, Hallowe'en, Valentine's Day, July 4th, etc., are mixed together in the party room and at the table. A "Real Crazy" centerpiece may be made of a watermelon, squash, eggplant or pumpkin, with rag-mop hair and construction paper features pasted onto three sides of the "head." Set the crowd to making "Real Crazy" masks (See Party Games, Mad Masks, Page 13) and then try a game of "Observations" on Page 12.

Whimsical, colorful birthday party themes for very young children include Mother Goose, Western Round-up, Fairyland, Doll Tea Parties, and, "bring your favorite stuffed animal to an Animal Party!"

14

RAINBOW BIRTHDAY CAKE

2 cups sifted cake flour	2 eggs, well beaten
2¼ tsp. baking powder	1 tsp. vanilla
1/2 tsp. salt	2/3 cup milk
1/2 cup shortening	Quick Fluffy Frosting
1 cup sugar	Colored marshmallows

Set oven for moderate, 350°. Grease two round, 8-inch layer cake pans. Sift together flour, baking powder and salt; set aside.

Cream shortening. Slowly add and beat in sugar; beat until well blended. Add eggs and vanilla; beat well. Add sifted dry ingredients alternately with the milk, a little at a time, and stir only until smooth after each addition. Turn batter into cake pans and bake 25 minutes or until golden. Cool cake slightly in pans on a rack. Remove from pans; cool on rack. Fill and frost layers with Quick Fluffy Frosting. Decorate with colored marshmallows, as shown in the picture.

QUICK FLUFFY FROSTING

In a bowl, stir together *1 egg white, 1 cup sugar* and *1/8 tsp. salt*. Stir in *1/2 cup boiling water* and beat rapidly with an electric mixer or a rotary beater until mixture holds a peak. Beat in *1/2 tsp. vanilla*.

15

TEEN AGE BIRTHDAY SUPPER

Assorted Sandwiches

Pickles   Olives   Celery

Real Crazy Cake*

Make Your Own Sundaes*   Milk

*Recipes on page 18.

REAL CRAZY CAKE
(see pic., page 16)

3 cups sifted all-purpose flour
2 cups sugar
6 Tbsp. cocoa
2 tsp. baking soda
1 tsp. salt

3/4 cup melted shortening
2 Tbsp. vinegar
2 tsp. vanilla
2 cups cold water
Chocolate Butter Frosting

Set oven for moderate, 350°. Mix dry ingredients together in mixing bowl; then sift into an ungreased 13 x 9 x 2-inch pan. With the back of a mixing spoon, make 3 depressions in the dry mixture; pour the shortening in one depression, vinegar in the second and vanilla in the third. Pour water over the top of the mixture. Mix and blend thoroughly until batter is smooth. Bake 50 to 60 minutes, or until cake springs back when lightly touched with fingertip. Cool slightly; remove from pan and cool on a rack. Frost with Chocolate Butter Frosting.

CHOCOLATE BUTTER FROSTING: In a bowl combine and beat *2/3 cup softened butter or margarine, 1/4 tsp. salt* and *1 cup sifted confectioners' sugar* until light and fluffy. Mix in *1 egg yolk* and *3 squares (1 oz. ea.) melted unsweetened chocolate.* Beat in *5 cups sifted confectioners' sugar* a little at a time, alternately, with *1/2 cup milk or light cream,* beating after each addition until smooth and creamy. Beat in *1 Tbsp. vanilla.* If thinner frosting is desired, add a little more *milk or cream* by teaspoonfuls.

MAKE YOUR OWN SUNDAES
(see pic., page 16)

Chocolate Sauce
Butterscotch Sauce
Frozen sliced strawberries, thawed
Frozen raspberries, thawed
Crushed pineapple

Ripe bananas
Assorted nuts
Maraschino cherries
Whipped cream
1/2 gal. tubs assorted ice creams

Arrange sauces, fruits and garnishes in serving dishes around tubs of ice cream. Have ice cream scoops and a variety of sundae and banana-split dishes ready for each guest to prepare his favorite combination.

CHOCOLATE SAUCE

Put *2 pkg. (2 cups) semisweet chocolate pieces* and *1 cup light corn syrup* in top of a double boiler. Heat, stirring constantly until blended. Stir in *1/2 cup evaporated milk, 2 Tbsp. butter or margarine* and *1 tsp. vanilla.* For a thinner sauce, add a little more *corn syrup.* Makes about 2 cups.

BUTTERSCOTCH SAUCE

In a saucepan, combine *2 cups brown sugar, 1/2 cup milk, light cream or evaporated milk, 6 Tbsp. light corn syrup* and *4 Tbsp. butter or margarine.*

Bring to a boil, stirring constantly, and cook about 3 minutes, or until mixture thickens. Remove from heat. Stir in *1/2 tsp. vanilla* and a *few grains salt*. Serve warm. Makes about 2 cups.

FOUR TiER CAKE
(see front cover)

5¾ cups sifted all-purpose flour	2½ cups milk
3¾ cups sugar	2 tsp. vanilla
3 Tbsp. baking powder	1/2 tsp. almond extract
2 tsp. salt	5 eggs
1⅓ cups soft shortening	Frosting (see note below)
	Pastel mints

Set oven for moderate, 350°. Grease and flour the pans of a 4-tier cake pan set: one pan 9 inches in diameter, one 7¼ inches, one 5½ inches and one 3¼ inches. Grease and flour cupcake pans for any remaining batter.

Sift together flour, sugar, baking powder and salt in a large mixing bowl. Add shortening to dry ingredients with about half the milk. Beat 2½ minutes at slow to medium speed with an electric mixer, or 375 vigorous strokes by hand. Scrape down bowl 2 or 3 times. Add remaining milk, vanilla, almond extract and eggs; beat 2½ minutes more, as above, until very smooth and creamy. Turn batter into cake pans, about 2/3 full. Any remaining batter may be baked in cupcake pans.

The easiest way to bake the 4 tiers is to chill the 2 smallest cakes and any cupcakes in the Fresh Food Compartment of your Foodarama until the 2 larger cakes are done. Bake the 9-inch cake about 55 minutes and the 7¼-inch cake about 40 minutes or until golden; remove from oven and cool. Then bake the remaining 2 cakes about 30 minutes and the cupcakes about 25 minutes or until done. Cool cakes slightly in pans on a rack. Remove from pans; cool on rack. Fill and frost cake. Decorate with pastel mints and candles, as pictured.

NOTE: Use your favorite cooked white frosting recipe, a packaged fluffy frosting mix, or the recipe for Quick Fluffy Frosting on page 15, doubling the amounts. If desired, mashed tart jelly may be used as filling between the layers instead of frosting.

ICE CREAM MOUNTAIN
(see front cover)

Choose several ice cream flavors and colors to blend with the party color scheme. To accompany the Four Tier Cake pictured, vanilla, pistachio and strawberry ice creams were used to match the mints and candles.

With an ice cream scoop or large round spoon, scoop out balls of ice cream and set side by side on a large tray. Freeze in the Freezing Compartment of your Foodarama until serving time. To serve, pile up ice cream balls on a large platter to resemble a pyramid or mountain. If desired, sprinkle a few of the top balls with shredded coconut to look like snow.

VALENTINE PARTY

Hearts and Cupids run rampant on February 14th! For a mood-setting Valentine Party invitation, make a construction paper heart of red, pink or white (See INVITATIONS, Page 6). The cover sparkles with matching sequins, perhaps a paper doily ruffle frames the cover, and inside is all of the party data. Decoration colors are red and white, or pretty pastels. Tiny red and white paper hearts flutter overhead, each one suspended by a thread which is Scotch-taped to the ceiling. Doorways become lovely archways of fluttering red cellophane hearts. Fresh flowers, leaves and tall red or white candles enhance the scene. As guests arrive, set them to making the most original valentine cards ever seen from materials which are laid out on a table—paper hearts, lace paper doilies, cupid cutouts, etc. Valentine-makers then exchange valentines, and escort partners to the party table.

The party table centerpiece may be either a pretty tray, or a "flower" heart. (Shape the outline of a heart from coat-hanger wire, and then cover the outline with fresh flowers using picture wire to secure them to the frame.) Fill the heart with silver foil-wrapped chocolate hearts, each one Scotch-taped onto a "stem" of coat-hanger wire which is secured at the base in a lump of clay or florists' base material. Lemon or lime leaves hide the wires. Sprinkle tiny red paper hearts over the table surface, paste a border of the same hearts to the tablecloth edge, and paste a single tiny heart to the corner of each guest napkin. For a place-card favor, wrap a little nut cup in red crepe paper, paste a white paper heart to the front, and fill the cup with valentine candies or red lollipops.

Play at least two games well-suited to your romantic theme. Try a "Famous Lovers" charade. Give each couple the names of a pair of famous lovers—Elizabeth Barrett and Robert Browning, Jack and Jill, Samson and Delilah—to act out its charade for the others to guess. Follow this with a more active game, "Elopement" (See Party Games, Page 13).

MILE HIGH RASPBERRY PIE
(see pic., page 22)

2 pkg. (10 oz. ea.) frozen raspberries
2 envelopes unflavored gelatin
1/2 cup sugar
1/2 cup water

4 egg whites, stiffly beaten
2 cups heavy cream, whipped
1 baked 9-inch pie shell
  (see note below)
Shredded coconut

Thaw raspberries; drain juice into a measuring cup; add cold water if necessary, to make 1 cup raspberry juice. Soften gelatin in the raspberry juice. Combine sugar and water; stir over low heat until sugar dissolves. Cook rapidly to 235° on candy thermometer, or until syrup spins a thread. Add softened gelatin to syrup; stir to dissolve. Slowly pour syrup mixture over egg whites, while beating rapidly. Continue beating until mixture forms peaks when beater is raised. Fold in cream. Fold in drained raspberries. Spoon into pie shell. Garnish with shredded coconut. Chill several hours, or until set.

NOTE: Prepare half the recipe for Pastry as given on page 28, or use a packaged pie crust mix. Line a 9-inch pan with the pastry and flute the edge. Prick entire surface with a sharp pointed fork. Bake in a hot oven, 450°, 12 to 15 minutes or just until golden. Cool thoroughly.

Claret Punch
(see pic., page 22)

1/2 cup fresh or frozen
  lemon juice
1 can (6 oz.) frozen pineapple
  juice, reconstituted

1 cup sugar
1 bot. (4/5 qt.) claret wine
2 bot. (28 oz. ea.) chilled ginger ale
Ice wreath of roses or block of ice

Combine fruit juices and sugar; stir until sugar dissolves. Add wine; chill mixture in the Fresh Food Compartment of the Foodarama. To serve, put ice wreath in a punch bowl. Pour fruit juice over the ice. Pour in ginger ale; stir gently. Makes 24 to 30 punch-cup servings.

ICE WREATH OF ROSES: Half fill a large ring mold or an angel food cake pan with ice water. Put the mold in the Freezing Compartment of your Foodarama until water is frozen. Make a pretty arrangement of sweetheart roses on top of ice. Add a thin layer of ice water and freeze quickly to hold roses in position. Fill mold with ice water and return to the Foodarama until frozen. To use, unmold and put bottom side up in the bowl of punch.

VALENTINE PARTY

Claret Punch*
Mile High Raspberry Pie*
Nuts   Mints
Coffee

*Recipes on page 21.

VALENTINE DINNER

Shrimp Cocktail
Roast Pork with Spiced Crabapples*
Sherry Glazed Yams*
Vegetable Medley Salad*   Hot Rolls
Banana Sea Foam*
Coffee

*Recipes on pages 24 and 25.

ROAST LOIN OF PORK

Select a loin of pork cut from the rib end, allowing one rib for each serving. Have the meatman saw between the backbone and the ribs for easier carving after roasting.

Wipe meat with a clean, damp cloth. Season with salt and pepper, if desired. Place meat, fat side up, on a rack in a shallow baking pan. Roast meat in moderate oven, 350°. Do not cover pan, add water, or baste meat. Allow about 35 minutes per pound for a roast from 3 to 5 pounds, and 30 minutes for a roast from 5 to 7 pounds. For best results, use a meat thermometer. Insert bulb so it rests in thickest part of meat without touching fat or bone. Thermometer should register 185° when done, regardless of weight. Pork must always be thoroughly cooked; there should be no trace of pink color.

Remove roast to a heated platter and garnish with sprigs of parsley and spiced crabapples.

Sherry Glazed Yams

Cook *6 large yams or sweet potatoes* in boiling, salted water. Peel; cut in quarters and arrange in a baking dish. Combine *1 cup sugar, 1/4 cup water, 1/4 cup sherry* and *1/4 cup butter* in a pan. Simmer 5 minutes. Pour over potatoes. Bake in a moderate oven, 350°, 30 to 45 minutes; turn several times. Makes 6 servings.

24

BANANA SEA FOAM

1 pkg. (3 oz.) lime-flavored gelatin
1 cup boiling water
1 pkg. instant vanilla pudding
1 cup milk

3 fully ripe bananas
1 Tbsp. lemon juice
1 cup heavy cream, whipped
Frozen strawberries, thawed

Dissolve the gelatin in the 1 cup water. Chill gelatin, stirring occasionally, until slightly thickened. Prepare pudding with the 1 cup milk. Combine gelatin and pudding. Mash bananas with a fork or rotary beater; blend in lemon juice. Combine bananas and whipped cream; fold into pudding mixture. Turn into a 1½-quart mold. Chill in the Fresh Food Compartment of your Foodarama until firm. Unmold on serving plate. Serve garnished with strawberries. Makes 8 servings.

VEGETABLE MEDLEY SALAD

Cook *2 packages (10 oz. ea.) frozen mixed vegetables* as directed on package. Drain and turn into a bowl.

Combine *1/2 cup salad oil, 2 Tbsp. vinegar, 1/2 tsp. garlic salt, dash of Tabasco sauce* and *1/4 tsp. paprika.* Beat with a rotary egg beater. Pour over the vegetables and toss to mix well. Chill in the Fresh Food Compartment of your Foodarama. At serving time, arrange on crisp lettuce on individual salad plates. Makes 6 servings.

WASHINGTON'S BIRTHDAY PARTY

This party has infinite possibilities for decoration and party atmosphere. An invitation in the shape of a hatchet sets the pace. Make it of white or red construction paper (See INVITATIONS, Page 6). Tack a pretty ribbon bow to the front, sew two tiny hatchet charms from the dime store to the ribbon ends.

Here's your chance to use those early American treasures for atmosphere—borrow them if you haven't enough of your own—teakettles, spinning wheels, kerosene lamps, copper and pewter accessories, candleholders, etc. Blue crepe paper streamers are overhead, clusters of white balloons hang down from them.

Pictures of the Presidents, or of famous men and women of American history, are on the walls, and may be used for quiz games; the guests guess their identities. As an ice-breaker, hold a "Cherry Hunt" for hidden red candies (See Party Games, Treasure Hunt, Page 12). At your party table, a "Cherry Tree" centerpiece immediately catches the eye. Secure a branch, which resembles the shape of a tree, in a flower pot of gravel. Real or construction paper leaves are wired on for foliage. Scotch-tape red cellophane-wrapped candies into little clusters, and paper-clip or wire the clusters to the "tree." Cover the pot with red crepe paper and add a few white paper hatchets.

For a more formal centerpiece, any handsome heirloom—a teakettle or apothecary jar—may be filled with red and white flowers. Or, winter wheat and grasses combined with a sparkling arrangement of shining red apples, nuts and white grapes, will be particularly attractive with copper or pewter antique pieces. Nut cups may be covered in blue or red crepe paper; add white paper hatchets to make them double as place-cards. Fill with silver foil-wrapped chocolate candies.

True or False Games, Naming the States and the Presidents, are good for these parties. (See Party Games, Page 12, for more game ideas.)

WASHINGTON'S BIRTHDAY DINNER
Planked Lamb Chops*
Duchess Potatoes*
Peas   Mushrooms
Assorted Rolls   Mint Jelly
Tossed Green Salad
Cherry Pie*   Coffee

*Recipes on pages 27 and 28.

PLANKED LAMB CHOPS

6 double loin lamb chops,
   boned and rolled
6 to 12 large mushroom caps

Melted butter or margarine
3 cups hot mashed potatoes or
   Duchess Potatoes
3 cups hot cooked, seasoned peas

Oil and heat a plank in a very slow oven, 250°. Remove plank and keep warm. Then, broil chops 15 minutes with top surface 3 inches below source of heat. Turn chops and broil 10 minutes longer.

Meanwhile, cook mushrooms in butter until golden. Place broiled chops on plank. Make a border of mashed potatoes using a pastry tube or two spoons; brush with butter. Return planked chops to broiler for about 5 minutes to lightly brown the potatoes. Spoon peas around chops; garnish with mushrooms. Serve at once. Makes 6 servings.

Duchess Potatoes

To *3 cups hot, seasoned mashed potatoes,* add and blend in *2 well-beaten egg yolks.* Force through a decorating tube onto a plank to make a border for planked chops, and brown as directed in recipe above. If desired, pile into a greased baking dish, or make individual mounds on a greased baking sheet and bake in a very hot oven, 450°, until brown. Makes 6 servings.

CHERRY PIE

2 cans (1 lb. ea.) red sour pitted, water-pack cherries	Dash cinnamon
	1 recipe Pastry
1/2 to 1 cup sugar	1 Tbsp. butter or margarine
1/4 cup flour	Sweetened whipped cream, if desired

Drain cherries and put into a bowl. Combine sugar, flour and cinnamon. Add to cherries; mix well. Roll out half the pastry and line a 9-inch pie pan; flute the edge. Roll out remaining pastry and cut a spray of cherries as shown to decorate pie. Set spray aside.

Pour cherries into pie shell; dot with butter. Place cherry spray cut-out on top. Bake pie in a hot oven, 400°, 35 to 40 minutes or until brown. Cool. Serve garnished with whipped cream.

PASTRY

2 cups sifted all-purpose flour	2/3 cup shortening
1 tsp. salt	5 Tbsp. cold water, about

Sift flour and salt together into a large mixing bowl. Cut in shortening with 2 knives or a pastry blender, until mixture resembles coarse corn meal. Sprinkle a tablespoon of cold water over mixture and toss with a fork to mix well. Repeat until dough is moist enough to hold together when pressed into a ball. Wrap in waxed paper; chill well in the Fresh Food Compartment of your Foodarama. Divide dough in half; roll out each half on a lightly floured board to desired size. Makes one 8 to 9-inch 2-crust pie or two 8 to 9-inch pie shells.

28

FESTIVE ICE CREAM ROLL

Confectioners' sugar
4 eggs
1 tsp. baking powder
1 tsp. vanilla

1/4 tsp. salt
3/4 cup granulated sugar
3/4 cup sifted cake flour
1 pint cherry vanilla ice cream

Set oven for hot, 400°. Grease bottom and sides of a 15 x 10 x 1-inch pan; line with waxed paper and grease lightly. Sift a little confectioners' sugar over a tea towel; shake off excess and set towel aside.

Beat eggs until foamy. Add baking powder, vanilla and salt; continue beating until very light. Beat in the granulated sugar, about 1 tablespoonful at a time. Beat until very thick. Fold in sifted flour, a little at a time. Pour into pan. Bake 13 minutes or until top springs back when lightly touched with fingertip. Loosen cake at once from pan with point of sharp paring knife. Invert onto towel. Remove pan; quickly remove waxed paper and trim off crisp edges with a sharp knife. Roll up cake from narrow end. Wrap towel tightly around roll; cool on a rack.

When cake is cool, soften ice cream slightly. Unroll cake carefully and spread at once with ice cream and roll up again. Serve at once sprinkled with confectioners' sugar, or freeze as directed below.

FOODARAMA FREEZING TIP: Wrap the ice cream roll in a polyethylene bag. Freeze in the Freezing Compartment of your Foodarama. Cake may be stored satisfactorily for 3 to 4 months. To serve, remove from freezer; let stand 5 minutes at room temperature. Unwrap; serve at once.

TEA PARTIES
Big and Little

The afternoon tea party may be big or little, simple or elaborate, but its format is always charmingly informal. As with Open House, guests arrive at any time within the prescribed hours, stay only as long as they wish, enjoy a single cup of tea or several, and depart whenever they please, with no fear of "breaking up the party." The tea table may be set formally or informally (Table Settings, Page 11, shows its proper service arrangement). Choice of table decorations is the hostess', although the dainty little tea cakes and sandwiches influence many hostesses toward a more delicate setting.

The centerpiece may be tall and striking in appearance, but should not overwhelm your attractive party foods. Delightful arrangements may be made of heirloom pieces—a teakettle, soup tureen or tall pitcher, filled with flowers or painted branches which have been dipped in glitter or tied with pretty bows. Old apothecary or candy stem-glasses, a single flower floating in each, are delicate and lovely for twin centerpieces. Tall, handsome candles are a must for the friendly, intimate scene.

The "Little Tea Party" service is brought in on a tray, to be served around a coffee or occasional table in the living room. The tray holds: pot of hot tea, pot of hot water, creamer, lump sugar and tongs, plate of lemon slices with fork, cups, spoons and dessert plates (saucers are optional; the cup may be placed on the dessert plate, the spoon placed behind the cup with its handle parallel to the cup handle), napkins and a little bud vase with a single flower. The tea snacks may be brought in by a friend, and served by the hostess.

TEA SANDWICHES

The sky is the limit for variety in party sandwiches: tiny closed and open-faced sandwiches, rolled sandwiches, pinwheels, cornucopias, ribbons and checkerboards. Use fresh or day-old white or whole wheat bread and remove all crusts. Thin-sliced bread is a must for all kinds of sandwiches, except checkerboard and ribbon. Cut the bread for open-faced or closed sandwiches in fancy shapes with cooky cutters, or make full size sandwiches and cut each finished sandwich into 3 or more small ones.

The butter and fillings must always be softened or moist enough so the bread will not tear in the spreading.

Closed sandwiches are made of 2 slices of bread with filling between: thinly sliced turkey, ham or cheese, thinly sliced tomato with mayonnaise or any of the fillings and butters suggested on page 55.

Open-faced sandwiches are made of one slice of bread, spread first with butter, then a filling, and garnished. Some garnishes to use are: chopped parsley or nuts; stuffed olive slices; bits of pimiento; minced egg white or sieved yolk; cream cheese edging put on with a pastry tube.

Directions for making pinwheels and ribbon sandwiches follow. On page 55 are suggestions for Party Sandwiches—fillings and seasoned butters. Try all these, then let your imagination take over.

PINWHEELS

Cut crusts from a loaf of unsliced day-old bread. Cut loaf in thin, lengthwise slices. Roll each slice with a rolling pin; spread with butter and soft cream cheese filling. Put a row of stuffed olives at the narrow end; roll the bread around the olives; wrap in waxed paper. Chill in the Fresh Food Compartment of the Foodarama. To serve, remove paper; cut in thin slices.

RIBBON SANDWICHES

Cut crusts from regular sliced white and whole wheat bread. Stack alternately 2 slices of each bread, spread with one or more fillings or butters. Wrap the sandwiches in waxed paper and chill in the Fresh Food Compartment of your Foodarama. At serving time, cut sandwiches, as shown.

31

PETITS FOURS

1 white sheet cake, 9 x 13 inches   Petits Fours Frosting
Apricot Glaze   Confectioners' Icing

Trim off outside edges of cake. Cut cake into squares, diamonds or rectangles, using a sharp knife. Brush off excess crumbs.

Spread top and sides of each cake with a thin layer of Apricot Glaze and place each one about 1 inch apart on waxed paper.

Place wire racks on top of some sheets of waxed paper or cooky sheets. When excess glaze has dripped off cakes, put them on prepared racks in rows about 2 inches apart and let stand to dry glaze. Using a tablespoon, spoon Petits Fours Frosting over cakes. Frosting should leave a coating about 1/16 inch thick. (Excess frosting will drip down on the paper or cooky sheet.) Scrape excess frosting off the paper; reheat and re-use until all cakes are frosted. Tint small amounts of the Confectioners' Icing various colors and decorate cakes, as shown, using wooden picks or a decorator's tube. Makes about forty 1½-inch squares.

Apricot Glaze

Put *1½ cups dried apricots* in a bowl. Cover with *cold water*. Let soak overnight. Drain apricots and press through a food mill or sieve. Measure apricots into a saucepan and add an *equal amount of sugar*. Stir to mix in sugar. Bring mixture to a boil over low heat, stirring constantly. Boil and stir 5 minutes. Remove from heat and cool. Use as directed.

Petits Fours Frosting

1½ cups granulated sugar   3/4 cup water
1/8 tsp. cream of tartar   1/2 tsp. vanilla
                                     Confectioners' sugar

Combine granulated sugar, cream of tartar, water and vanilla in a saucepan. Cook and stir sugar mixture over low heat until sugar dissolves. Then bring to a boil, without stirring, and boil to 226° on a candy thermometer. Cook to lukewarm (85°). Add and stir in just enough confectioners' sugar to make a good pouring consistency. Pour over cakes, tipping the rack so each cake is coated uniformly.

Confectioners' Icing

Measure *1 cup confectioners' sugar* into a bowl. Stir in just enough *water, about 1 Tbsp.*, to make frosting easy to force through a decorating tube. Or add a little more water if it is to be used for making lines with a toothpick. Tint as desired. Makes about 1/2 cup.

SCOTCH SCONES

3 cups sifted all-purpose flour
2 tsp. baking powder
1 cup sugar
1/4 tsp. salt

3/4 cup butter or
   margarine, softened
1 cup chopped seedless raisins
1 egg, well beaten
Milk

Set oven for very hot, 450°. Grease a large cooky sheet.

Sift together flour and next 3 ingredients into a large bowl. Cut butter into flour mixture. Add raisins; stir to mix well. Pour egg into a measuring cup; add enough milk to make 1 cup. Stir egg-milk mixture into flour.

Turn dough out on lightly floured board or pastry cloth; knead lightly 15 to 20 turns or 1/2 minute. Roll out dough about 3/4 inch thick. Cut into triangles with floured knife. Place about 1/2 inch apart on cooky sheets. If desired, brush tops with a mixture of 1 slightly beaten egg yolk and 2 tablespoons water. Bake 10 to 12 minutes or until brown. Makes about 24 scones.

BRIDGE for the LADIES

Afternoon bridge may be preceded by a luncheon consisting of a main hot dish, salad, dessert and coffee, or the hostess may prefer to serve only a rather special dessert with coffee. Early afternoon bridge may also be followed by a light salad, a sandwich or dessert, and coffee.

LOBSTER NEWBURG

2 cups cooked lobster meat
1/3 cup butter or margarine
2 Tbsp. flour
1/3 cup sherry
4 egg yolks, slightly beaten

2 cups light cream or milk
1/2 tsp. salt
Few drops Tabasco sauce
Few grains nutmeg
6 slices toast

Cut lobster into bite-size pieces. Melt butter in a saucepan; add lobster. Heat and stir over low heat for 2 minutes. Sprinkle with flour; mix well. Slowly stir in sherry; heat 2 to 3 minutes. Combine egg yolks and cream; mix well. Slowly stir into lobster mixture. Continue heating and stirring over low heat until mixture thickens. Do not boil. Stir in salt, Tabasco sauce and nutmeg. Serve on toast. Makes 6 servings.

PARTY SANDWICH LOAF

1 small round loaf white bread	Avocado Filling
Softened butter or margarine	Cream cheese, about 1/2 lb.
Ham and Celery Filling	Light cream
Curried Egg Filling	Sliced stuffed olives
2 tomatoes, thinly sliced	Sprigs of parsley

Cut loaf, crosswise, into four thick slices. Spread each slice with butter. Spread bottom slice with Ham and Celery Filling. Top with second bread slice; spread with Curried Egg Filling. Top with slices of tomato and third bread slice. Spread with Avocado Filling; top with remaining bread slice. Mash cream cheese; stir in enough cream so cheese will spread easily; beat until smooth. Spread on top and sides of loaf. Garnish with olive slices and parsley. Cut into wedges to serve. Makes about 12 servings.

HAM AND CELERY FILLING: Combine *1 cup ground cooked ham, 1/2 cup finely chopped celery* and enough *mayonnaise* to moisten.

CURRIED EGG FILLING: Combine *4 finely chopped hard-cooked eggs, 1/2 tsp. curry powder* and enough *mayonnaise* to moisten.

AVOCADO FILLING: Mash *2 fully ripe avocados;* add *2 Tbsp. highly seasoned French dressing.* Stir until well blended.

FROZEN FRUIT AND CHEESE SALAD

1 tsp. unflavored gelatin
2 Tbsp. cold water
1 large pkg. (1/2 lb.) cream cheese
1/4 cup mayonnaise
1/4 tsp. salt
1/8 tsp. paprika

1 cup drained, canned crushed
  pineapple
1/4 cup diced maraschino cherries
1/2 cup chopped toasted almonds
1/2 cup heavy cream
Watercress or lettuce

Sprinkle gelatin over the cold water; let stand to soften. Set over hot water; stir until gelatin dissolves. Put cheese in a bowl; mash with a fork. Add mayonnaise, salt and paprika; whip until fluffy. Combine pineapple, cherries and almonds. Stir into cheese mixture. Whip cream until stiff; fold into cheese mixture. Spoon into 8 to 10 individual molds. Freeze in the Freezing Compartment of your Foodarama until firm. Unmold salads on a serving plate or individual plates. Garnish with watercress. Makes 8 to 10 servings.

Biscuit Tortoni

1/2 tsp. unflavored gelatin
1 Tbsp. cold water
3/4 cup sugar
1/2 cup hot water
6 egg yolks, well beaten

2 cups heavy cream
2 tsp. vanilla
3/4 cup finely chopped toasted
  almonds
3/4 cup finely crushed macaroon crumbs

Soften gelatin in cold water. Combine sugar and hot water in a saucepan. Stir over medium heat until sugar dissolves; boil to 238°, or until a little syrup forms a soft ball when dropped into cold water. Slowly pour and stir mixture into egg yolks; stir until mixture cools slightly.

Add gelatin to egg mixture and stir until gelatin is dissolved; cool well. Whip cream; fold into egg mixture with remaining ingredients. Spoon into small paper cups. Freeze in the Freezing Compartment of your Foodarama until firm. Makes about 12 servings.

GALA CAKE

1/2 cup frozen diced pineapple
1/2 cup frozen diced peaches
1/2 cup seedless grapes
1/4 cup halved maraschino cherries
1 cup heavy cream

Confectioners' sugar
1/2 tsp. orange extract
1/2 tsp. lemon extract
2 8 or 9-inch yellow
    cake layers (see tip below)

Thaw and drain frozen fruits. Add grapes and cherries. Whip cream; sweeten to taste with confectioners' sugar. Fold in flavoring extracts, then the drained fruit. Fill and frost cake layers with the whipped cream-fruit mixture as pictured. Garnish with additional fruit, if desired.

Choco-Cream Cake

Soften *1 tsp. unflavored gelatin* in *2 Tbsp. cold water.* Dissolve softened gelatin over boiling water. Mix *1/2 cup confectioners' sugar* and *1/4 cup breakfast cocoa;* stir into *1 cup heavy cream.* Add dissolved gelatin to cream; stir to blend. Whip until thick; chill in the Fresh Food Compartment of your Foodarama before using. Use the mixture to frost tops of two 8 or 9-inch white cake layers.

FOODARAMA FREEZING TIP: The cake may be baked ahead of time, then wrapped and frozen in the Freezing Compartment of your Foodarama until the day of the party.

BRIDAL SHOWERS

Traditionally, the Shower is a surprise to the honored guest. Keeping the secret may require supreme effort on the part of her good friends, but when "she" innocently agrees to stop by Ann's house to help hang new draperies and arrives to find, in place of draperies, a full-blown party in *her* honor, that look of pleased astonishment is well worth everyone's effort! Although plans for the party may be carried out by a single hostess or a committee of two or three, the shower for the Bride-to-Be is often hosted by all of her closest friends. Once the gift category (kitchen, serving equipment, living-room accessories, etc.) has been decided, make a list of all the gift possibilities, plus a price maximum. Each friend may then select from the list the article she wishes to buy to avoid duplication.

When the guest-of-honor arrives, the party theme is obvious. Perhaps the party rooms are decorated in wedding-cake colors, or to represent the month in which her wedding will be held. Flowers, balloons, bride and groom figurines and "wedding ring" designs (see Anniversary Parties, Page 52) set the scene: wall-mounted snapshots, borrowed from her family's and friends' photo albums, tell the honored guest's life story to date, from baby days to dating days with ex-boyfriends.

The luncheon table holds a centerpiece of a doll's house encircled by a "garden" of fresh flowers. Ribbons run from under the house to each placecard-favor which can be an inexpensive, doll-house plastic accessory—refrigerator, sink, chair, etc. — on which a guest's name has been painted. Or a miniature bridal bouquet-corsage of tiny flowers and leaves, framed with a paper doily and tied with narrow ribbon, makes a delightful favor. When luncheon is over, the gifts are presented in a prettily-decorated gift wastebasket or breadbox. After the gifts are opened, test the Bride-to-Be in the housewifely arts: have her thread a needle, sew on a button, chop a green pepper, peel an onion, etc., while wearing boxing gloves! When the other guests roar, let them try, too!

BRIDAL SHOWER LUNCHEON

Chicken Bouillon
Shrimp Portuguese*
French Fried Potato Puffs*
Sliced Tomato Salad   Hot Biscuits
Baked Alaska*
Coffee or Tea

*Recipes on pages 39 and 40.

SHRIMP PORTUGUESE

2 lb. frozen raw shrimp	3/4 tsp. salt
1/2 cup butter or margarine	1/8 tsp. pepper
1 clove garlic, minced	1/2 cup minced parsley

Peel and devein shrimp; wash and dry with paper towels.

Melt butter or margarine in a skillet over medium heat. Add garlic and salt and cook until golden brown, stirring occasionally. Add shrimp; cook just until underside turns pink. Turn and cook until pink on other side, about 10 minutes in all. Add pepper, additional salt if desired, and parsley. Cook 1 minute longer. Makes 6 servings.

FRENCH FRIED POTATO PUFFS

2 cups mashed potatoes	1 cup sifted all-purpose flour
4 slices crumbled crisp bacon	2 tsp. baking powder
2 eggs, well beaten	1 tsp. salt
	Fat or cooking oil

Combine potatoes, bacon and eggs in a bowl. Sift together flour, baking powder and salt. Stir into potato mixture; blend well. Heat fat or pour cooking oil into a deep fryer or heavy kettle to a depth of 2 inches; heat to 375°. Drop potato mixture by spoonfuls into hot fat. Fry 3 minutes or until brown. Drain. Makes 6 servings.

BAKED ALASKA

1 yellow sheet cake, about 1 inch thick
2 pt. brick ice cream, any flavor

5 egg whites
2/3 cup sugar

Set oven for very hot, 450°. Remove ice cream from cartons and return to the Freezing Compartment of the Foodarama. Lay cartons on cake, end to end; cut cake 1/2 inch larger, on all sides, than the cartons. Place cake on a wooden board or cooky sheet covered with brown paper.

Whip egg whites until stiff but not dry; gradually beat in sugar, a little at a time; continue beating until smooth and glossy. Place ice cream on top of the cake. Quickly spread meringue over top and sides of ice cream and cake; make sure they are completely covered. Bake 5 minutes or until meringue is golden brown. Remove Alaska carefully onto a chilled serving platter using 2 spatulas and serve at once. Makes 8 to 12 servings.

FOODARAMA FREEZING TIP: Cake may be baked ahead, then wrapped and stored in the Freezing Compartment of the Foodarama with the ice cream. Use your own recipe or a 17 to 20-oz. package of yellow cake mix baked as directed in a 13 x 9½ x 2-inch pan. Prepare meringue; bake just before serving.

Flaming Alaska

Prepare Baked Alaska, above, reserving the egg shells. Select 3 or 4 shells which have been evenly broken; carefully wash and dry shells. Before placing Alaska in oven, insert shells, cut side up, in the meringue. Bake as directed. Pour a tablespoon of hot brandy into each shell; ignite and bring to the table flaming.

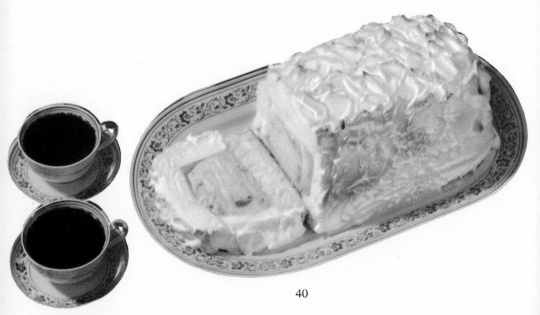

BABY SHOWERS

One of every hostess' favorite guests-of-honor is the dear friend who is soon to have a baby. No males welcome at this intimate occasion, the Baby Shower, except perhaps the Father-to-Be who arrives when the fun is over, given a pat on the back and the gifts of his important lady to carry home.

Compare notes on "who brings what" to avoid duplication in the gift department. The Mother-to-Be must be brought to the party-house on a ruse since the surprise element is half the fun.

The party rooms are decorated with flowers and leaves, borrowed baby dolls, and that age-honored symbol, the stork. So simple that a child can make them, you will be able to turn out a flock of storks in no time. Refresh your memory with a peek at a good dictionary or encyclopedia illustration, then copy the outline of the stork onto a shirt cardboard (don't bother to draw the legs). Cut out your outline. Scotch-tape two legs of coat-hanger wire onto the body, then cover each side of the cardboard with a thin layer of cotton (glue on); also glue on two black button eyes. Crayon the bill yellow, stand the stork in two fat gumdrops or two lumps of modeling clay. The birds may range from 3-inch-high placecards to 10-inch-high table and room decorations.

If you plan to key your table decoration to your menu's main dishes, use a simple fruit or vegetable centerpiece, but dot with some of the little storks and several of those very inexpensive, dime-store, tiny plastic baby dolls. For a more elaborate table-setting, use any pastel color scheme. The centerpiece might then be a doll's cradle or crib filled with pretty flowers and leaves. Add a miniature plastic crib or cradle at each place-setting as a favor-placecard, and fill each with two or three flowers. Or set one of your taller storks into a tray of fresh flowers, and surround him with the same little baby dolls. A smaller stork-favor holds a flower (Scotch-taped on) in his bill. After luncheon, bring in the gifts in a gaily decorated baby carriage or cradle.

PARTY CHICKEN

3½ lb. ready-to-cook chicken,
    cut up
2 cups boiling water
2 Tbsp. chili powder
1/4 tsp. pepper
1/4 tsp. cinnamon
2 Tbsp. grated onion
1 tsp. salt

1/4 cup fat
2 cups unsweetened pineapple juice
2 cups thawed frozen
    pineapple chunks
2 fully ripe bananas, sliced
    lengthwise
1 ripe avocado, sliced
1/2 lb. seedless white grapes

Put chicken in a deep kettle; add next 6 ingredients. Cover and simmer
1 hour. Remove chicken from broth. Reserve broth. Heat fat in a skillet.
Brown chicken on all sides; arrange in baking pan. Add pineapple juice
to broth; heat and pour over chicken. Arrange pineapple chunks over
chicken. Bake in moderately hot oven, 375°, 30 minutes. Lift chicken
and fruit onto a serving dish; garnish with the remaining fruit. If desired,
thicken the gravy with several tablespoons of flour which have been
blended with a little water. Serve gravy separately. Makes 6 servings.

ANGEL FOOD CAKE

1 cup sifted cake flour	1 tsp. cream of tartar
1/4 tsp. salt	1 tsp. vanilla
1 cup egg whites	1¼ cups sugar
(7 or 8 medium-size eggs)	

Set oven for moderately low, 325°. Sift flour; measure and sift 4 times more.

Add and stir salt into egg whites; whip until frothy. Sprinkle cream of tartar over egg whites and continue to whip until they hold soft, moist peaks. Fold in vanilla. Gradually beat sugar into egg whites, 2 tablespoons at a time. Sift a small amount of the flour over egg mixture and gently fold in; continue until all flour is added. Turn into an ungreased 9-inch tube pan. Bake 1 hour and 15 minutes or until top springs back when lightly touched with fingertip. Invert pan; allow to cool completely in this position. Loosen cake from sides and tube of pan with a spatula. Frost with Pastel Frosting, or sprinkle with confectioners' sugar.

PASTEL FROSTING

Combine *1/3 cup tart jelly* (plum, currant or grape), *1 egg white* and *few grains salt* in the top of a double boiler. Whip with a rotary beater until mixed. Put over boiling water and continue to beat constantly 3 minutes or until frosting stands in peaks. Cool and spread on cake.

EASTER

Celebrate this most joyous of springtime holidays with an Easter Brunch after Sunday services. Inside the house, your guests are greeted by an array of toy bunnies in nests of pastel-tinted eggs, and delicate spring flowers everywhere. To cut flower costs, make bouquets of only a few blossoms along with many handsome, inexpensive greens—even single blossoms in striking containers can be very effective.

While you are making last-minute preparations in the kitchen, your guests create fantastic Easter Bonnets for the Easter Parade to come later. On a previously prepared work table are these materials: shirt cardboards, crepe paper in assorted colors, paper doilies, artificial flowers, real fruits and vegetables, feathers, veiling, sequins, paste and scissors, narrow elastic, needles and threads. Let the gentlemen design bonnets while the ladies decorate hard-cooked, tinted eggs with crayons, paints, gummed tape and stars, paper doilies, scraps of felt and veiling, paste and scissors. These, too, are judged after Brunch, following the Easter Parade in which the lads must model their creations.

Time for Brunch, and whether you serve at a buffet, sit-down luncheon table or card tables, color adds to the springtime mood. Green, yellow and white are the traditionally popular Easter colors, but many hostess' color choices range from lavender to red-checked gingham at these informal brunches. Centerpiece possibilities are endless: Perch a huge chocolate bunny in a bed of Easter "grass," and surround it with pretty tinted eggs. Make a miniature garden of tinted halves of broken egg shells; place a marshmallow into each shell, stick colored wooden picks into it, and top the picks with "flowers" of Easter egg candies and gumdrops. Base the shells on a mirror surrounded with "grass." Or try a handsome basket or bowl filled with pastel-tinted eggs, a different color for each guest. Tie a color-matched ribbon around each egg, and run a ribbon to each place-setting where it is tied around a second egg of the same color, and on which a guest's name is printed with crayon.

PARTIES

Children will love a centerpiece of a bunny dressed in a gay, crepe paper Easter outfit with fancy, matching bonnet. For children too, bunny favors are made by sliding marshmallows onto a lollipop stick to cover. White paper ears, lined with pink paper, are glued onto the cellophane paper covering the lollipop. Add glued-on whiskers of waxed white thread. Bits of gumdrops make the features, gumdrop feet and tail are held on by toothpicks. Finish off with a jaunty pink ribbon, tied around his neck.

For children or adults, glue Easter "grass" around the outsides of nut cups, add pipe cleaners for basket handles, and fill with Easter candies. Or make little Easter baskets of small boxes covered with crepe paper (tie on a ribbon handle). One of these little baskets at each place-setting can serve a threefold purpose: print a guest's name on the side for a placecard; place a gift-wrapped token present inside for a favor; and later use the basket to hold Easter eggs and candies found in the Treasure Hunt.

The Hunt may be indoors or out, and may be made more suspenseful by hiding a few, very special silver-paper-covered chocolate eggs among the others. Or start the group of searchers off with a written clue which will lead them on to the next clue, and so on. The final clue leads them to a cache under the party table where chocolate bunnies for all have been hidden. Now the guests are ready to rest up while they make Easter Cards or play other games adapted to the Easter theme (see Party Games, Page 12).

Your Easter dinner setting has a pretty lace or organdy-over-linen cloth. Matching glass holders of tall, white candles and a handsome glass bowl filled with tinted, glitter-dipped Easter eggs are arranged down the table center on a runner of Easter "grass" or cellophane which you have shredded. Miniature chocolate Easter eggs, wrapped in jewel-colored metallic paper, are sprinkled liberally over the grass. At each place-setting, the placecard-favor is a tiny potted plant or flower, with each guest's name written on a pot in black or white ink.

HOT CROSS BUNS

1 cup milk
1/3 cup butter or margarine
1/2 cup sugar
1½ tsp. salt
1/4 cup warm (not hot) water

2 pkg. active dry yeast
5 cups sifted all-purpose flour, about
2 eggs, beaten
Melted shortening
1 cup golden raisins
Confectioners' Icing

Scald milk in a saucepan. Add butter, sugar and salt; stir until sugar dissolves. Cool to lukewarm. Measure warm water into a large bowl. Sprinkle in yeast and stir until dissolved. Add lukewarm milk mixture. Add 2½ cups of the flour; beat until smooth. Stir in eggs. Add 2½ cups more flour or enough to make a soft dough; mix well. Knead about 10 minutes. Place dough in a greased bowl; brush with shortening. Cover; let rise in a warm place until doubled in bulk, about 2 hours. Punch down. Turn out on floured board; knead in raisins. Pinch off pieces of dough and shape into 1½-inch balls. Place in greased pans, 1 inch apart. If desired, brush with egg yolk diluted with a little water. Cover and let rise until doubled in bulk, about 1 hour. Bake in moderately hot oven, 375°, 30 minutes. Cool. Make crosses on buns with Confectioners' Icing (see recipe on page 33). Makes about 24 buns.

PANETTONE
(see pic., page 48)

1/2 cup milk	2 eggs, beaten
1/2 cup butter or margarine	4 cups flour, about
1/4 cup sugar	1/3 cup seedless raisins
1 tsp. salt	1/4 cup mixed, diced candied fruits
1/4 cup warm (not hot) water	1/4 cup canned, diced toasted almonds
1 pkg. active dry yeast	1 Tbsp. grated lemon peel

Scald milk. Cool to lukewarm. Cream butter with sugar and salt. Measure the warm (110°) water into large mixing bowl. Sprinkle yeast over water; stir until dissolved. Stir in milk and the butter mixture. Add eggs and about half the flour. Beat until smooth. Blend in next 4 ingredients. Add enough remaining flour to make a soft dough. Turn out on lightly floured board; knead until smooth and elastic. Place in greased bowl; brush top with shortening. Cover with a damp cloth; let rise in a warm place until doubled in bulk (about 1½ hours). Punch down. Turn out on lightly floured board. Let rest 10 minutes. Shape into a round loaf. Place in a greased, deep round pan. (You can use a 2½-qt. cooking pot.) Cover; let rise in a warm place until doubled in bulk, about 1 hour. Cut an "X" across the top. If desired, beat an egg yolk slightly; stir in a little water and brush top of dough with the mixture. Bake in a moderately hot oven, 375°, 50 to 60 minutes or until brown.

FOODARAMA FREEZING TIP: You can bake the Panettone ahead of time, wrap it and freeze it in the Freezing Compartment of your Foodarama.

Baked Ham Slice
(see pic., page 48)

Select a center cut ham slice, about 4 inches thick, from an uncooked ham. Bake in a moderately low oven, 325°, allowing about 30 minutes per pound. Forty-five minutes before end of baking time, remove ham from oven. Cut gashes in the fat; baste ham with a little peach or apricot marmalade. Return to oven until done; baste several times with ham fat.

Remove to a platter and garnish with canned pear halves tinted with green food coloring, and topped with preserved ginger or tart jelly.

Eggs Marguerite
(see pic., page 48)

Set oven for moderate, 350°. Separate 9 eggs, taking care to keep the yolks unbroken. (Drop each yolk into a separate custard cup.) Add 1/2 tsp. salt to egg whites and whip until stiff but not dry. Turn into a baking dish. With a teaspoon, make 9 hollows in the top of the whites; drop an egg yolk in each. Bake 10 minutes or until yolks are set and whites are delicately browned. Makes 9 servings.

EASTER BRUNCH

Orange Juice
Eggs Marguerite*
Baked Ham Slice with Pear Garnish*
Panettone*
Assorted Jams, Marmalades, Preserves
Coffee

Recipes on page 47.

EASTER DINNER

Fruit Cup

Crown Roast of Lamb*

Oven Browned Potatoes   Green Peas

Lettuce with Blue Cheese Dressing

Watermelon Pickle   Hot Rolls

Mint Ice Cream Pie*   Coffee

*Recipes on pages 50 and 51.

CROWN ROAST OF LAMB

1 double crown roast of lamb (14 to 17 ribs) filled with ground lamb
3 to 4 cups soft bread crumbs
1/4 cup butter or margarine, melted
1½ tsp. salt
Few grains pepper
1 medium onion, chopped
2 stalks celery, minced
2 cups canned crushed pineapple
Water

Remove ground meat from center of roast. Cook ground meat in a skillet over low heat until it loses its pink color. Stir and break it into small pieces with the side of a spoon as it cooks. Drain fat off meat and discard. Add next 7 ingredients to cooked meat; toss with two forks to make a stuffing. If stuffing is not moist enough, add a little water until ingredients hold together. Form part of the stuffing into small balls, one ball for each rib. Chill balls. Fill center of crown with remaining stuffing. Place roast on rack in open pan. Cover tips of ribs with foil to prevent burning.

Roast lamb in moderately low oven, 325°, about 4 hours. During last 45 minutes of cooking time, remove foil and place meat balls on tips of ribs. When roast is done, remove to chop plate. If desired, garnish lamb as shown, with pineapple chunks and parsley, and decorate top of roast with slices of sautéed lamb kidneys. Makes about 8 servings.

MINT ICE CREAM PIE

1 qt. pkg. chocolate
   chip-mint ice cream

Vanilla Crumb Crust
3 egg whites
1/2 cup sugar

Pack ice cream into crumb crust. Place in the Freezing Compartment of the Foodarama. About half an hour before serving time beat egg whites until very foamy. Slowly add and beat in sugar; beat until whites form stiff, shiny peaks. Remove pie from freezer and top with meringue. Be sure to cover ice cream completely, pressing meringue against crust to seal. Bake in a very hot oven, 500°, 2 to 3 minutes. Serve at once.

VARIATION: Any desired flavor or a combination of flavors of ice cream may be used in place of chocolate chip-mint, if preferred.

VANILLA CRUMB CRUST

Mix *1¼ cups crumbs* (30 vanilla wafers) and *1/4 cup soft butter or margarine* until crumbly; press on bottom and up sides of 9-inch pie pan, forming a small rim. Bake in a moderately hot oven, 375°, 8 minutes; cool. Makes 1 shell.

WEDDING ANNIVERSARIES

There are some exceedingly wise and happily married hostesses who place their own wedding anniversaries at the very top of their parties-to-give lists. From the first through the sixtieth, anniversaries are perfect excuses for party-times.

According to tradition, each anniversary has a particular symbol which often determines the type of gift given (see below). Party room and dinner table decorations may be keyed to the specific anniversary, or be designed around your menu's handsome dishes as in Sea Food en Coquilles. Any well-stocked aquarium or pet shop has fascinating marine decorations—lacy sponges, intricate coral formations, handsome sea shells. Combine several of these with flowers or greens for an original centerpiece; place your candles in interesting old bottles; set all onto a fish-net tablecloth.

You may want to emphasize a wedding ring motif. Pattern the wall behind the buffet table with large rings made of coat-hanger wire and covered with aluminum foil. Repeat the motif with smaller rings suspended over the party table. Around a flower centerpiece, place the names of the honored couple. Cut tall letters out of shirt cardboard, cover each with glue, and dip into silver glitter. Surround each candle base with a ring.

Adapt these same ideas for the anniversary reception for a very large gathering. Since the reception is often preferred by couples celebrating 25th or 50th anniversaries, it approximates their wedding reception in that as many as possible of the original wedding party are again in evidence. The honored couple stand in line "to receive" their guests; the buffet table is handsomely set to hold beautiful flowers and candelabra, the punch bowl and the cake which is once more cut by the "bride."

ANNIVERSARY SYMBOLS: 1st anniversary, paper; 2nd, cotton; 3rd, leather; 4th, fruits and flowers; 5th, wood; 6th, candy; 7th, wool or copper; 8th, rubber or electrical; 9th, willow or pottery; 10th, tin; 20th, china; 25th, silver; 50th, gold.

ANNIVERSARY DINNER

Sea Food en Coquilles*
Roast Turkey*
Mashed Potatoes   Asparagus
Hot French Bread   Assorted Relishes
Cake   Ice Cream
Coffee

*Recipes on pages 53 and 96.

SEA FOOD EN COQUILLES

1 cup water	1 pkg. (8 oz.) frozen scallops,
2 tsp. lemon juice	thawed and thinly sliced
Butter or margarine	1 cup flaked cooked crabmeat
1/2 lb. mushrooms, sliced	1 cup diced cooked lobster meat
1 cup dry white wine	1 cup deveined cooked shrimp
1 small onion, sliced	1/4 cup flour
1/2 bay leaf	Few grains pepper
6 sprigs parsley	6 Tbsp. grated Gruyère cheese
1 tsp. salt	1 cup bread crumbs

Combine water, lemon juice and 2 tablespoons butter in a pan. Add mushrooms; simmer 10 minutes. Drain the liquid from the mushrooms. Set the mushrooms and liquid aside.

Put next 5 ingredients in a pan. Bring to a boil. Add scallops and simmer 10 minutes. Lift out onion, bay leaf and parsley and discard. Drain liquid from scallops; add to liquid from mushrooms. Combine scallops with crabmeat, lobster and shrimp.

Measure 2 cups of the combined liquids, adding water if necessary. Melt 1/4 cup butter in the top of a double boiler. Blend in flour and pepper. Slowly stir in the 2 cups liquid. Cook over low heat, stirring constantly, until thick and smooth. Add cheese; stir until it melts. Place over hot water and cook 15 minutes. Stir shellfish and mushrooms into sauce; add more salt if desired. Heat well. Fill scallop shells with the mixture; sprinkle with crumbs; dot with butter. Brown in a preheated broiler. Makes 10 to 12 servings.

ANNIVERSARY BUFFET

Fruit Cup
Chicken Salad Tarts*
Parsley Buttered Potatoes
Brussels Sprouts with Almonds*

Hot Rolls   Currant Jelly

Coffee   Cake   Mints

*Recipes on page 54.

CHICKEN SALAD TARTS

2 pkg. pie crust mix	1½ cups mayonnaise
1 green pepper, diced	3/4 tsp. salt
1½ cups diced celery	Few drops Tabasco sauce
3 cups diced, cooked chicken	1½ tsp. Worcestershire sauce

Prepare pie crust mix as directed on package; chill in the Fresh Food Compartment of your Foodarama. Combine remaining ingredients. Roll out pastry; use a little more than half and roll out 1/8 inch thick on lightly floured board. Cut 4 circles, 7 inches in diameter. Fit loosely into four 6-inch pie pans; trim edges. Fill pans with chicken mixture. Roll out remaining pastry. Cut in 4 circles, 6 inches in diameter. Cut out centers with a cooky cutter; scallop, if desired. Put pastry on pies; trim and press edges together. Bake in hot oven, 425°, 20 to 25 minutes, or until pastry is golden. Serve hot. Makes 4 servings.

Brussels Sprouts with Almonds

Cook frozen Brussels sprouts in salted water until tender. Drain. Pour over melted butter or margarine and toasted slivered almonds. Toss lightly.

ANNIVERSARY CAKE

ANNIVERSARY RECEPTION

Party Sandwiches*
Champagne Punch*
Anniversary Cake*

Ice Cream   Coffee

Nuts   Assorted Mints

Recipes below.

The cake for a wedding anniversary is just as important as it was at the wedding. It should be tiered and decorated, of course. Use the recipe for Four Tier Birthday Cake (see page 19). Frost it with white icing or, if you prefer, tint the icing a pastel color to match other decorations.

Crown the cake with the traditional miniature bride and groom dolls, the one from the wedding cake if it is available. Use other decorations to fit the anniversary, such as gold wrapped coins for a fiftieth; tiny china dishes for the twentieth; flowers and marzipan fruits for the fourth.

Party Sandwiches

Make a variety of tiny sandwiches using directions for Tea Sandwiches on page 31. Suggestions for fillings and seasoned butters follow.

FILLINGS: Minced chicken, ham or sea food, and pickle relish with salad dressing; chopped dates and nuts with lemon juice; peanut butter and chopped preserved ginger; sieved egg yolk, anchovy paste and salad dressing; cream cheese and jam; jellies. See freezing tip, below.

SEASONED BUTTERS: Softened butter or margarine with enough of any of the following to taste: prepared mustard; horse-radish; anchovy paste; dried parsley leaves; onion juice; grated Parmesan cheese.

FOODARAMA FREEZING TIP: Make sandwiches ahead of time and freeze them in the Freezing Compartment of the Foodarama until needed. Sandwiches should be spread first with butter or margarine, then with the filling. Use fillings made of minced chicken, ham or other meat, sea food, egg yolks and peanut butter. Salad dressing is better than mayonnaise for these fillings. Stay away from fillings made with hard-cooked egg white, chopped celery, or a large proportion of cream cheese, jelly or jam.

Champagne Punch

1 pkg. (10 oz.) frozen strawberries	1 bot. (4/5 qt.) sparkling burgundy
2 tsp. grated lime peel	1 bot. (4/5 qt.) dry champagne
Juice of 1 lime	1 bot. (4/5 qt.) sauterne
Ice Wreath of Roses (see page 21)	Whole strawberries, lime slices

Combine first 3 ingredients in a saucepan. Simmer 10 minutes, stirring often; put through a sieve. Chill in the Fresh Food Compartment of your Foodarama. Just before serving, put ice wreath in a punch bowl. Pour strained fruit juice over ice. Add wines and stir gently. Garnish with whole berries and lime slices. Makes about 25 punch-cup servings.

BUFFETS

The buffet luncheon or dinner is the perfect answer for novice or busy hostesses, or for that entertaining dilemma, the two-small dining room vs. the too-long guest list. Your most important consideration in buffet-dining is the menu, for buffet service demands easy-to-eat "fork" foods. No steaks, roasts or other foods difficult to cut, and bread and rolls are pre-buttered.

See Table Settings, Page 9, for tips on table placement and setting. Guests serve themselves, or a friend may assist by serving the hot dishes at the table. If the food and company are of the best, no guest will mind the informal "stand-up-to-dine" arrangement of large buffet parties. If you have enough chairs, individual "lap trays" are an asset (each tray holds a complete place setting) and they are easy to manage. Little stack tables, placed near chairs, are also convenient. Or simply clear off coffee and occasional tables so guests may rest dinner plates or cups and saucers on their surfaces. If there is ample space, set up bridge tables and cover with little tablecloths and miniature centerpieces to complement the main buffet table.

Take your decorative theme from the occasion itself. Centerpiece and candles for the table placed against a wall are set toward the back of the table. With a center of the room table placement, the centerpiece may go to the table corner, ends or center. Try seasonal leaves, ferns or evergreens arranged around the bases of a row of graduated candles; a handsome pair of hurricane lamps filled with flowers; a pretty basket overflowing with shining vegetables—eggplant, red and green peppers, tomatoes, squash, etc.; a fine glass punch bowl filled with cat-tails, seed pods and winter grasses. Confetti, paper cut-outs —"snowflakes" or "pumpkins" or "stars"— sprinkled over the tablecloth, add a party touch. Narrow satin or paper ribbon, draped along the cloth edges, add color and festivity.

HAWAIIAN CHICKEN CURRY

2 cups Coconut Milk
1/3 cup butter or margarine
1/2 cup minced onion
1/3 cup flour
4 tsp. curry powder
1 tsp. salt
1/8 tsp. pepper

1/4 tsp. ginger
2 cups chicken stock
3 cups diced, cooked chicken
1 cup drained, frozen pineapple chunks
Hot cooked rice
Chutney, raisins, shredded
   coconut and peanuts

Prepare Coconut Milk as directed below. Melt butter in a saucepan. Add onion; cook until soft but not brown. Blend in next 5 ingredients. Slowly stir in Coconut Milk and chicken stock. Bring to a boil, stirring constantly. Reduce heat to low and continue to cook and stir until mixture thickens. Stir in chicken and pineapple; heat thoroughly. Serve over hot rice with chutney, raisins, shredded coconut and peanuts on the side. Makes 6 to 8 servings.

COCONUT MILK: Put *4 cups grated, fresh coconut or 2 packages (4 oz. ea.) shredded coconut* in a bowl. Pour *2 cups hot milk* over coconut; let stand 30 minutes. Put a double thickness of cheesecloth in a strainer over a bowl. Turn mixture into cheesecloth and press to remove all liquid; discard coconut. Chill until ready to use. Makes 2 cups milk.

FLANK STEAK WITH FRUIT STUFFING

2 flank steaks (equal in size), about 1½ lbs. each Fruit Stuffing	1/4 cup shortening Salt and pepper 1/2 cup water

Lay one flank steak on top of the other, narrow ends together. Skewer edges of steaks together at one-inch intervals with round wooden picks along sides and narrow ends; leave wide end open. Lace twine around picks to close edges to make a "pocket." Fill pocket with Fruit Stuffing. Then skewer opening; lace closed and tie.

Melt shortening in a large skillet; add meat and fry over medium heat, turning once to brown evenly. Season with salt and pepper to taste. Reduce heat to low. Add water and simmer, covered, 1½ hours or until meat is tender. Remove skewers and twine before serving. Makes 6 to 8 servings.

FRUIT STUFFING

1/4 cup finely chopped onion 3 cups 1/2-in. soft bread cubes 3/4 tsp. salt	1/2 tsp. poultry seasoning 1 cup diced, fully ripe banana 1/2 cup butter or margarine, melted

Combine all ingredients except butter. Toss lightly with two forks. Sprinkle butter over mixture and toss to mix thoroughly.

SKEWERED OYSTERS

1 pt. shucked oysters
Sliced bacon, cut in
   1-in. pieces

18 mushroom caps
Melted butter or margarine
Saffron Rice

Preheat broiler and broiler pan. Drain oysters well. Thread oysters, bacon and mushroom caps, alternately, on 6 skewers; brush with butter. Place on pan. Broil until bacon is crisp; turn once. Make a bed of Saffron Rice on a large platter; arrange skewers on top. Makes 6 servings.

SAFFRON RICE

6 cups water
1½ tsp. salt

1½ cups rice
1/4 tsp. saffron, about
1/3 cup butter or margarine

Put water in a 2-quart saucepan. Add salt and heat to boiling over high heat. Gradually stir in rice. Add saffron and stir well; cover and turn heat to low. Cook, stirring occasionally, until rice is tender and liquid is absorbed. Add butter and toss lightly with a fork to mix well. Makes about 6 cups.

STRAWBERRY SHORTCAKE

2 pkg. (10 oz. ea.) frozen strawberries
2 cups sifted all-purpose flour
3 tsp. baking powder
1/2 tsp. salt

2 Tbsp. sugar
1/2 cup shortening
1 egg, well beaten
1/2 cup milk, about
Whipped cream

Partially thaw the strawberries.

Sift together flour, baking powder, salt and sugar into a bowl. Add shortening and cut in with a pastry blender or 2 knives. Combine egg and milk; stir into flour to make a soft dough. Turn out on a lightly floured board; knead gently 15 to 20 turns. Roll out dough 1/2 inch thick. Cut out 2-inch rounds using a floured cutter and place 1/2 inch apart on an ungreased cooky sheet. Bake in a very hot oven, 450°, 12 to 15 minutes or until biscuits are brown. Cool slightly.

Split cooled biscuits. Put lower halves on serving plates and spoon berries on top. Then cover with remaining biscuit halves and the berries; garnish with whipped cream. Makes 8 servings.

60

BROWNIE PUDDING

1 cup sifted all-purpose flour
2 tsp. baking powder
1/2 tsp. salt
3/4 cup granulated sugar
2 Tbsp. cocoa
1/2 cup milk
1 tsp. vanilla

2 Tbsp. melted shortening
3/4 to 1 cup chopped nuts
   (walnuts or pecans)
3/4 cup firmly packed brown sugar
1/4 cup cocoa
1¾ cups hot water
Vanilla ice cream or sweetened
   whipped cream

Set oven for moderate, 350°, and grease an 8 x 8 x 2-inch pan.

Sift together the flour, baking powder, salt, granulated sugar and the 2 tablespoons cocoa. Slowly stir in milk and vanilla; mix just until smooth. Stir in melted shortening, blending well. Add and stir in nuts. Turn into the greased pan.

Mix together the brown sugar and the 1/4 cup cocoa; sprinkle evenly over batter in pan. Pour hot water over the top. Bake 45 minutes. Serve warm with ice cream or whipped cream. Makes 8 to 10 servings.

FOR A GLORIOUS FOURTH

For your own Independence Day buffet, or for that big, back-yard share-party with friends and neighbors, stars and stripes set the theme. Fold a sheet of white notepaper in half for an easy-to-make invitation; paste a tiny flag or blue and red gummed stars to the cover.

Spread your party table with a white cloth, sprinkled with red, blue and silver stars; or use a red, white and blue cloth especially made for this occasion, but suitable for so many more parties. Fat, red firecracker twin-centerpieces are made by rolling two shirt cardboards into tubes and covering each completely with red crepe paper (short pieces of rope make the fuses). Surround each firecracker with white candles which are sprinkled with more tiny stars, and cover both centerpiece and candle bases with a layer of fresh-cut red and white flowers. Miniature versions of the firecracker make delightful little favors if they are filled with candies. An Uncle Sam hat made of shirt cardboard, colored crepe paper, stars and Scotch tape, may be placed upside down to become a flower-holder centerpiece. Make little Uncle Sam hats for candy baskets, add pipe cleaner handles which are stapled on. Early American dolls or figurines are charming little conversation pieces if placed attractively among the serving dishes on clusters of leaves or aluminum-foil stars. History-minded guests will also enjoy an early American model cannon centerpiece, surrounded by little tin soldiers and tiny flags (base in gumdrops).

From old magazines, cut out pictures of scenes and people, famous in American history; remove all identifying captions. Mount each picture nicely, and hang on the wall behind the buffet table (or on a wire stretched between two trees, for an outdoor party). Guests will enjoy testing their knowledge. If games are played, historical charades on famous quotes or incidents, played by couples or small groups, are fun. For outdoor celebrations, traditional races and relays are perfect (See Party Games, Page 12).

DEVILED DRUMSTICKS

8 to 10 chicken drumsticks
  and thighs
1/2 cup butter or margarine
1 clove garlic, cut in half
1/2 tsp. salt
1/4 tsp. savory
1/8 tsp. pepper
2 cups cornflake crumbs

Wash and dry chicken. Melt butter or margarine with garlic, salt, savory and pepper in medium-size saucepan. Dip chicken pieces one at a time, first in butter mixture, then in crumbs, coating each piece well. Arrange chicken in a single layer in a large shallow baking pan. Remove garlic, then pour remaining butter mixture over chicken. Bake in a moderate oven, 350°, 1 hour or until crispy brown and tender when pierced with a fork. Makes 8 to 10 servings.

Blueberry Muffins
(see pic., page 64)

1/4 cup shortening
1/3 cup sugar
2 eggs, well beaten
2 cups sifted all-purpose flour

4 tsp. baking powder
3/4 tsp. salt
2/3 cup milk
2/3 cup blueberries

Set oven for hot, 400°. Grease muffin pans. Beat shortening until creamy; add sugar gradually, continuing to beat. Stir in eggs. Sift together 1⅔ cups of the flour, baking powder and salt. Add flour mixture alternately with milk to egg mixture. Stir just enough to moisten dry ingredients. Mix blueberries with remaining 1/3 cup flour; gently stir into batter. Spoon into pans. Bake 30 minutes or until brown. Makes about 14 muffins.

FOODARAMA FREEZING TIP: Both Deviled Drumsticks and Blueberry Muffins may be made ahead of time, wrapped and put in the Freezing Compartment of the Foodarama ready for serving. On the day of the party, thaw the Drumsticks and Muffins to serve cold or at room temperature, or heat to serve warm.

STARS 'N' STRIPES SUPPER

Deviled Drumsticks*
Sky Rocket Relish Bowl*
Potato Vegetable Salad*
Blueberry Muffins*
Strawberry Ice Cream Meringues*
Pink Lemonade*

*Recipes on pages 63 and 66.

POTATO VEGETABLE SALAD
(see pic., page 64)

6 cups potato salad
(see note below)
1 pkg. (10 oz.) frozen mixed
vegetables, cooked

1/4 cup French dressing
Lettuce or other salad
greens
Paprika

Chill potato salad in the Fresh Food Compartment of the Foodarama. Drain cooked mixed vegetables; toss with French dressing; chill. Combine potato salad and marinated vegetables, tossing lightly to distribute vegetables. Serve on lettuce or other greens. Sprinkle with paprika. Makes 8 to 10 servings.

NOTE: Use your favorite potato salad recipe or use the recipe for Golden Potato Salad on page 74.

SKY ROCKET RELISH BOWL
(see pic., page 64)

Fill a salad or relish bowl about 2/3 full with crushed ice. Stand green onions upright in center of ice. Arrange overlapping slices of tomato and cucumber in a circle around onions.

STRAWBERRY ICE CREAM MERINGUES
(see pic., page 64)

6 egg whites
Few grains salt

1 cup sugar
1 qt. strawberry ice cream
Frozen sliced strawberries

Set oven for very low, 275°. Place 2 sheets of unglazed paper on 2 cooky sheets. Whip egg whites with salt until stiff but not dry. Add sugar, a little at a time, beating well after each addition. Beat until meringue holds very stiff, glossy peaks. Drop meringue onto paper; shape into small bowls or nests 3 inches apart, on the paper. Bake 1 hour or until meringue is a delicate brown. Remove from paper at once and place on serving plates. Fill with generous scoops of ice cream. Top with frozen sliced strawberries which have been partially thawed. Makes about 12 servings.

NOTE: A packaged meringue mix may be used, if desired, for making the meringue shells. Follow package directions for preparing and baking. Fill with ice cream and strawberries. One package (about 4 oz.) meringue mix makes 8 shells.

PINK LEMONADE
(see pic., page 64)

Combine *2 cups fresh, frozen or canned lemon juice, 2 tsp. grated lemon peel* and *1½ cups sugar;* stir well or shake until sugar dissolves. Add *grenadine syrup* by spoonfuls to tint a deep pink. For each serving, pour approximately 1/4 cup lemon mixture over ice cubes in a tall glass. Fill glass with water. Makes 8 to 10 tall drinks.

CHOCOLATE CREAM DESSERT

1 pkg. (6 oz.) semisweet
   chocolate pieces
6 eggs, separated
1½ tsp. vanilla

18 lady fingers
1 cup heavy cream, chilled
3 Tbsp. chocolate syrup,
   see note below

Melt chocolate in the top of a double boiler over hot water. Add egg yolks, one at a time, beating well after each addition. Add vanilla and stir well. Whip egg whites until stiff but not dry. Fold in the chocolate mixture.

Line a loaf pan with strips of waxed paper, allowing it to extend over top edges of pan. Split lady fingers and place a layer on bottom and around sides of pan. Spoon in half the chocolate mixture. Top with another layer of split lady fingers; spoon in remaining chocolate mixture and top with remaining split lady fingers. Chill dessert in the Fresh Food Compartment of your Foodarama several hours or until firm.

Just before serving, whip the cream. Fold in chocolate syrup, a tablespoon at a time. Lift dessert from the pan, using edges of waxed paper and a spatula; place on a serving dish. Remove the paper. Frost the dessert with whipped cream mixture. Makes 8 servings.

NOTE: In place of chocolate syrup, you may use 2 Tbsp. each of confectioners' sugar and cocoa.

SUMMER FUN
with BARBECUES

Casual, modern living at its best! Food, cook and guests move outdoors and savor the special delights that occur only when meat, flame and summer breeze combine!

Grilled Lobster Tails

Buy lobster tails, weighing about 1/2 lb. each. Allow 1 lobster tail per serving. Slit undershells of tails, lengthwise, with scissors to prevent curling. Run long skewers, lengthwise, through tails as shown. Melt some butter or margarine and brush on slit sides.

Put lobster tails, shell side down, on grill; barbecue over medium heat about 15 minutes. Brush slit sides with more melted butter and turn. Grill lobster tails about 3 minutes more or until done. Shell will be bright red when lobsters are done. Serve piping hot with melted butter and lemon wedges, if desired.

KEBOBS AND LAMB CHOPS

Double rib lamb chops,
   cut about 2 inches thick
Zucchini

Cherry or bell tomatoes
Mushrooms
Cooking oil

Allow 1 or 2 lamb chops per serving. Have the meatman French or trim the meat from the ends of the bones.

Wash the zucchini and tomatoes well. Cut the zucchini in pieces, 1½ inches long. Wash mushrooms and trim stems to within 1/4 inch of caps. Peel caps if necessary. Starting with the zucchini, thread the vegetables on long skewers; add a firm cherry tomato and a mushroom cap and repeat as shown. Brush the vegetable kebobs with cooking oil.

Start barbecuing the lamb chops on the grill over medium heat. Barbecue them about 15 minutes and turn. Then lay the skewered vegetables on the grill; continue to barbecue the chops and the vegetable kebobs about 15 minutes longer or until done as desired, turning the vegetable kebobs frequently and brushing them with more cooking oil as required.

FOODARAMA FREEZING TIP: Frozen meats must be thawed and brought to room temperature before barbecuing them.

BARBECUED WHOLE CHICKENS

Buy 2 to 3½-lb. ready-to-cook roasting chickens. Allow 1/2 bird per serving. Wash chickens; pat dry. Put 2 to 3 tsp. salt in body cavity of each chicken. Skewer neck skin to back skin of each bird, and loop heavy twine around at least twice to keep wings flat against body. Tie legs and tail together with heavy twine. Dovetail birds on the spit rod; insert spit forks. Balance birds on rod and tighten fork-screws securely. Insert a barbecue thermometer so tip rests in thickest part of the thigh. Brush chickens with cooking oil.

Attach spit to unit. Put a drip pan under birds. Start the motor. Spit barbecue chickens over medium heat until done, brushing often with more oil. Allow about 20 minutes per pound barbecuing time; thermometer should read 190°. If desired, brush birds with Cranberry Spice Glaze the last 10 to 15 minutes of barbecuing.

Cranberry Spice Glaze

Combine *1 cup mashed, jellied cranberry sauce, 1/3 cup firmly packed brown sugar, 1/4 tsp. each mace and cinnamon* in a saucepan. Heat and stir until sugar dissolves. Makes enough for 3 chickens.

BARBECUED EYE OF ROUND

Buy a beef eye of round, weighing about 5 pounds. Allow about 1/3 pound per serving. Have the meatman wrap the beef in suet and secure with heavy twine. Put the meat on the spit rod and insert a spit fork at either end. Insert a barbecue thermometer in thickest part of meat as shown. Prepare the Wine Basting Sauce.

Put drip pan underneath the meat. Attach spit to unit; start motor. Spit barbecue beef over medium heat, basting often with Wine Basting Sauce. Allow 10 minutes per pound to barbecue meat. Thermometer should read 150° for medium-rare beef. When done, slice meat and serve.

Wine Basting Sauce

Put *1 cup red or white wine, 1/2 cup cooking oil, 1 teaspoon oregano, 1 clove garlic, crushed* and *2 small bay leaves* in a pint-size, screw-top jar. Cover jar; shake well to mix. Store sauce in the Fresh Food Compartment of your Foodarama until ready to use; shake sauce well before using. May also be used as a marinade. Makes about 1½ cups.

BARBECUED CLUB STEAK

Select club steaks cut 1½ inches thick. Allow 1 steak per serving.

Place steaks in a shallow pan. Pour Spicy Marinade on top. Cover pan and chill steaks in the Fresh Food Compartment of your Foodarama 3 to 4 hours, turning several times. Drain meat well.

Rub grill with cooking oil or a piece of fat. Lay steak on grill and sear 2 to 3 minutes. Then place steak over medium heat and continue barbecuing. Barbecue 6 to 10 minutes for rare steak and turn.

Sear second side of steak 2 to 3 minutes; place over medium heat as directed above and continue to barbecue 6 to 10 minutes longer for rare, or a little longer time per side for medium or well-done steak.

Spicy Marinade

Combine *1 cup wine vinegar, 1 cup cooking oil, 1 cup water, 1/4 cup minced onion, 3 bay leaves* and *6 to 8 whole cloves.* Put marinade in a screw-top jar; cover and store in the Fresh Food Compartment of your Foodarama until ready to use. Shake vigorously before using. Makes 3¼ cups.

PROSPECTOR HAM

1½ to 2-lb. center-cut
   precooked ham steak

1/2 cup pineapple juice
Fruit Kebobs

Rub a skillet with a small piece of ham fat. Slash fat edge of ham slice at 1/2-inch intervals; place in skillet. Pour pineapple juice over ham. Cook over medium heat 10 to 12 minutes. (Pineapple juice should evaporate during cooking.) Turn ham and continue to cook 10 to 12 minutes more or until lightly browned. Serve with Fruit Kebobs. Makes 4 servings.

Fruit Kebobs

2 red apples
2 ripe bananas

3 fresh apricots
8 pineapple chunks, drained
Melted butter or margarine

Cut 8 slices from apples as shown in picture. Peel bananas and cut in fourths, crosswise. Halve and pit apricots. On each of 4 skewers, arrange fruits beginning and ending with apple. Brush with butter. Lay kebobs on grill over medium heat. Cook, turning often, 20 to 25 minutes or until fruit is well heated. Brush often with more butter. Makes 4 servings.

SPARERIBS ON A SPIT

Meaty spareribs

Oriental Spice Mixture
Bottled barbecue sauce, if desired

Allow about 1 pound ribs per serving. Rub both sides of ribs with Oriental Spice Mixture. Put ribs into a shallow container. Let stand several hours at room temperature. Drain ribs before putting them on the spit rod. To put ribs on rod, run spit rod through center of rack starting at narrow end and lacing rod between bones. Lace second rack on rod starting at the wide end; continue until all spareribs are on spit rod. Insert spit forks and tighten. Then run several metal skewers through the ribs on outer edges to hold them securely.

Attach spit rod to unit. Put a drip pan under meat. Start the motor. Barbecue ribs over medium heat 45 minutes to 1 hour or until done. If desired, ribs may be brushed with a barbecue sauce during last 10 or 15 minutes of barbecuing time.

Oriental Spice Mixture

Combine *3/4 tsp. turmeric, 2 tsp. paprika, few grains dry mustard, 2 Tbsp. salt* and *1½ cups sugar* in a large screw-top jar. Shake to mix well. Makes 1½ cups.

CORN BARBECUED IN FOIL

Use fresh, young tender sweet corn or thawed corn on the cob from the Freezing Compartment of your Foodarama. Allow 1 to 2 ears corn per serving. If fresh corn is used, strip off husks and remove silk. Brush corn with softened butter or margarine and season with salt and pepper, if desired. Lay each ear on a double thickness of aluminum foil and sprinkle with a little water. Wrap foil securely around corn. Grill corn over medium heat, turning it often to cook evenly, about 20 minutes.

Barbecued Potatoes

Select medium-size potatoes. Scrub well and dry. Rub skins with soft butter or margarine. Wrap each potato tightly in a double thickness of aluminum foil. Lay potatoes directly on top of hot coals. Barbecue medium-size potatoes, turning occasionally, 45 to 60 minutes. Potatoes are done if they feel soft when gently pressed with an asbestos-gloved thumb. When soft, slit the foil, cut potato diagonally as shown. Press gently to break open. Season to taste with butter or margarine, salt and black pepper. Top each potato with a spoonful of sour cream and sprinkle with chopped chives.

GOLDEN POTATO SALAD

Combine *4 cups diced, cold boiled potatoes, 1 small chopped onion, 2 Tbsp. chopped parsley, 1 cup chopped celery* and *1 tsp. salt.* Pour *Mustard Salad Dressing* on top and stir gently until well mixed. Chill salad in the Fresh Food Compartment of your Foodarama. Arrange salad on *lettuce.* Makes 6 to 8 servings.

MUSTARD SALAD DRESSING: Combine *4 Tbsp. yellow prepared mustard. 2Tbsp. evaporated milk, 2 Tbsp. sugar, 2 Tbsp. vinegar, 1/4 tsp. salt* and *a dash pepper* in a bowl. Beat with a rotary beater until light and fluffy. Makes about 2/3 cup dressing.

Curried Rice Salad
(see pic., page 78)

(see pic., page 78)

4 cups hot cooked rice
1/4 cup French dressing
3/4 cup mayonnaise
2 Tbsp. minced onion
3/4 tsp. curry powder
1/2 tsp. salt

Few drops Tabasco sauce
1/2 tsp. dry mustard
1 cup diced celery
1½ cups cooked peas
Crisp salad greens
2 to 3 tomatoes, cut in wedges

Combine rice and French dressing; cool to room temperature. Mix together mayonnaise with next 5 ingredients. Put celery and peas in a large bowl. Pour in mayonnaise mixture. Add rice; toss lightly to coat. Chill in the Fresh Food Compartment of your Foodarama. Turn into a salad bowl. Garnish with salad greens and tomato wedges. Makes 6 servings.

Sea Island Grapefruit

For each serving put several thawed, drained frozen grapefruit sections on a double thickness of heavy-duty aluminum foil. Sprinkle fruit generously with brown sugar and light rum. Add a dash of cinnamon and 1 tsp. of butter or margarine. Wrap fruit securely in foil.

Barbecue foil-wrapped grapefruit on grill over medium heat 12 to 15 minutes or until grapefruit is well heated.

Fruit Spear Platter

A beautifully arranged platter of fresh fruit spears is simple to prepare and adds interesting color and texture to your barbecue fare. Prepare a Fruit Spear Platter as follows: On a bed of crisp salad greens arrange finger-size pieces of chilled watermelon, pineapple, cantaloupe or honeydew melon and bananas, thin unpeeled slices of red apples and quartered, cored, unpeeled pears; place a small whole pineapple in center of the platter, if desired. Provide small bowls of French dressing, sour cream and mayonnaise for "dunking," if desired.

PICNIC TIME

Signs of spring—balmy breezes, sunny days and the first robin—all point to packing up the picnic baskets with lots of goodies for a day out of doors. Keep baskets and supplies handy for pičnics until chilly fall breezes blow.

SANDWICH TIPS

Frozen sandwiches or fillings (see suggestions for fillings below) waiting to be thawed, or a variety of sliced cold cuts are perfect for that "spur of the moment" picnic. Add an easy-to-handle salad such as the Curried Rice Salad, pictured below, a beverage and cookies and you are ready to go.

MINCED CHICKEN FILLING

In a bowl, combine *2 cups minced cooked chicken, 1/3 cup salad dressing, 2 Tbsp. pickle relish* and *1 Tbsp. grated onion.* Makes 2 cups.

LAMB FILLING

In a bowl, combine *2 cups minced cooked lamb, 1 tsp. salt, 1/4 tsp. pepper, 1/4 cup capers, 3 tsp. chopped mint* and *1 Tbsp. lemon juice.* Makes about 2¼ cups.

SEA FOOD FILLING

In a bowl, combine *2 cups chopped cooked lobster, 1 cup chopped cooked shrimp, 1/3 cup finely chopped walnuts* and *1 medium-size cucumber,* finely chopped. Add enough salad dressing to hold ingredients together. Makes about 3 cups.

TUNA FILLING

In a bowl, flake contents of *1 can (7 oz.) tuna fish.* Add and mix in *3 table-spoons chopped pickle,* and *3/4 cup drained crushed pineapple.* Moisten the mixture with *a little French dressing.* Makes about 1 cup.

CRAN-APPLE FILLING

In a bowl, combine *1 cup cranberry sauce, 2 cups applesauce, 1/2 cup chopped Brazil nuts* and *1/4 tsp. ground cloves.* Makes 3½ cups.

PACKING POINTERS

Freeze the basic sandwich fillings in freezer containers in the Freezing Compartment of your Foodarama and leave the trimmings to add just before serving. Foods such as lettuce, chopped celery, tomato slices, jams, jellies and mayonnaise do not freeze well. Use cooked salad dressing if you combine all the filling ingredients before freezing.

Prepare and freeze sandwiches several days to a week ahead of time in the Freezing Compartment of your Foodarama. Use an air-tight wrap such as freezer paper or aluminum foil to prevent sandwiches from drying out. Label sandwich wrap including name of filling and date and, perhaps, the person it's for.

Salads such as potato or rice are improved by chilling. So prepare and chill them in the Fresh Food Compartment of your Foodarama several hours before packing them.

If you're carrying meat or other frozen foods a distance, freeze it first in the Freezing Compartment of your Foodarama and let it thaw on the way. Place pieces of waxed paper between each hamburger before wrapping. They'll separate more easily.

If the trip's a long one, keep chilled foods cool by wrapping packages in extra layers of newspaper or foil. Put them in a corrugated box with packages of frozen foods tucked in between until you get there. Then unpack and let the foods thaw.

PARTIES FOR SMALL FRY

TODDLERS Two, three or four guests at this age are enough, and as they arrive, let them play with a few toys. Then Mother leads a "Clapping March" to the party table (all step high and clap hands). A placecard made of a single lollipop, based in a fat gumdrop, holds a taped-on card with each child's name. A cluster of balloons forms the centerpiece; these are handed out to the guests. At each place are a little plastic dish and cup which later will be taken home as part of the party "loot." Play Ring Around the Rosie, Farmer in the Dell; read a simple story; play-act nursery rhymes with gestures and sound effects.

SIX-YEAR-OLDS A Costume Circus Party is perfect for this age group. Your party room and table are under the "Big Top" with crepe paper streamers hung from ceiling center to the sides of the room. Add a menagerie, stuffed animal toys in "cages" made of cartons with paper ribbon "bars," and circus pennants. At the table, a Circus Cake is the star. Each chair has a tied-on balloon which bears a guest's name, printed in white paint. A popcorn-ball clown favor has gumdrop features, and an upside-down ice cream cone hat, topped with a gumdrop "pom-pom." A Peanut Treasure Hunt, bubble-blowing and relay races are good activities.

TEN-YEAR-OLDS These young dynamos like action. Try a warm-weather, outdoor Scavenger Hunt, or an Athletic Party with a Three-Legged race, Circle Games, Volleyball with a balloon and Silly Skill games in which contestants pick up beans, peel oranges and tie knots while wearing work gloves. Winter skating or sledding parties are always favorites. Come home to finish off the party amid decorations to suit the occasion. Serve refreshments in great abundance, and simmer down your guests before sending them home by letting them make "Mad Masks" (see page 13).

FROSTED CHOCOLATE DROPS

1½ cups sifted cake flour
1½ tsp. baking powder
1/2 tsp. salt
1/2 cup shortening
1 cup sugar
2 eggs, slightly beaten

3 squares (1 oz. ea.)
   unsweetened chocolate, melted
1 tsp. vanilla
3/4 cup seedless raisins
1/2 cup milk
Easy Frosting

Sift together flour, baking powder and salt; set aside. Cream shortening thoroughly; gradually beat in sugar and continue beating until well blended. Add eggs and chocolate; beat well. Stir in vanilla and raisins. Add sifted dry ingredients alternately with the milk, a little at a time, and blend well. Cover and chill about 1 hour in the Fresh Food Compartment of the Foodarama.

Set oven for moderate, 350°. Grease cooky sheets.

Drop dough by rounded teaspoonfuls onto cooky sheets, about 2 inches apart. Bake 12 to 15 minutes. Remove from pans; cool on wire racks. When cold, spread with frosting and decorate, if desired, with colored candy sprills. Makes about 5 dozen.

EASY FROSTING

Put *2 cups sifted confectioners' sugar* in a bowl. Stir in enough *hot milk* (about 2 Tbsp.) to give mixture a good spreading consistency. Blend in *1 tsp. vanilla.* Divide into 3 parts. With a few drops food coloring, tint each batch the desired color.

CIRCUS CAKE

Set oven for moderately low, 325°. Grease a 12-inch spring form pan. Prepare 2 pkg. (17 to 20 oz. ea.) of your favorite cake mix, one at a time, according to package directions. Pour batter into the pan. Bake 1¼ hours or until done. Cool cake slightly; remove from pan and cool on a rack. Frost cake with Butter Frosting (see page 92) tinted tan.

Decorate animal crackers with melted chocolate applied with a wooden pick, making spots on leopards, stripes on tigers, manes on lions, etc.

Insert a ring of colored cocktail picks 2 inches from edge of cake, as shown. Sprinkle green sugar inside of ring. Arrange animals in the ring and around the edge of cake. Stand a cardboard ringmaster in the center.

Popcorn Balls

8 cups popped corn	1/4 cup water
1 cup sugar	2 tsp. vinegar
1/2 cup molasses	1/4 tsp. salt
	1 Tbsp. butter or margarine

Put corn into a large mixing bowl. Combine next 5 ingredients in a deep saucepan. Stir over low heat until sugar is almost dissolved. Cover; slowly bring to a boil. Remove cover. Boil rapidly, stirring constantly, to 270° or until a small amount of syrup turns slightly brittle when dropped in cold water. Remove from heat at once. Stir in butter. Pour in a fine stream over the popped corn, tossing constantly with a fork to coat all corn evenly. Grease hands lightly. Quickly shape into balls. Makes 8 to 12 balls.

BROWNIES

1/4 cup butter or margarine	1/4 tsp. salt
2 squares (1 oz. ea.) unsweetened chocolate	1 egg, unbeaten
3/4 cup sifted cake flour	1 cup sugar
1/2 tsp. baking powder	2 Tbsp. water
	1/2 tsp. vanilla
	3/4 cup chopped walnuts

Melt butter and chocolate together over hot water; cool slightly. Sift together flour, baking powder and salt; set aside.

Combine egg and sugar in a bowl; beat until well blended. Stir in chocolate mixture, water and vanilla, blending thoroughly. Add sifted dry ingredients and stir just until smooth. Mix in walnuts. Turn batter into a greased 8-inch square pan. Bake in a moderately low oven, 325°, 25 minutes or until top forms a dull crust which dents a little when lightly touched with fingertip. Cool slightly on a wire rack. Cut into bars, 1 x 4 inches, and remove from pan; cool. Makes 16.

Chocolate Milk

Add *1½ to 2 Tbsp. chocolate syrup* to *1 cup milk* for each serving desired. Beat with a rotary egg beater. Serve cold.

CHOCOLATE FLOAT: Drop a spoonful of vanilla, chocolate or coffee ice cream into each glass of Chocolate Milk just before serving.

TEEN AGER PARTIES

Turn that casual Teen-Age Get Together into a really festive occasion by serving the abundant party fare attractively, by dressing yourself prettily and by decorating your party room with plants, fresh flowers and soft lights. Whether you have refreshments around the coffee table, at card tables, or in the kitchen, party-up your serving with whatever inspiration you can find right in the house—a bread basket filled with gleaming red and green peppers, a pretty bowl filled with green leaves.

SLUMBER PARTIES can be tops even if guests bunk on floor pallets. Borrowed sleeping bags are perfect, and can tee off a "camping out" theme with fake, silver-foil moon and stars dangling from the ceiling, and a flashlight "campfire" around which you tell horror stories, of course. Add a Treasure Hunt (naturally, in the dark) for a midnight box snack of sandwiches, fruit, cookies, etc. (one box per guest), and don't forget that back-to-civilization breakfast for your ravenous "campers."

AFTER THE GAME PARTIES can be fun whether the team has won or lost. Is it basketball or football? If football's your game, a gallery of famous football heroes hangs on the wall; cut out newspaper pictures of top players, let the guests guess their identities. Your own football hero decorates the table — a football wearing crepe paper features, rag-mop hair and a helmet. Paper football cut-outs and school pennants pattern your tablecloth.

GRADUATION PARTIES use that impressive high school diploma to set the theme for party refreshments and decorations. A placecard "diploma" is made from a sheet of fine writing paper; roll and tie with a ribbon which holds a miniature ball-point pen. Write each guest's name on a "diploma." For your centerpiece, use a bowl of flowers surrounded by single flowers to be used as corsage and boutonniere favors.

JAM SESSION HAMBURGERS

One pound of ground beef makes 5 hamburgers. Plan on 2 to 3 hamburgers for each "customer." In addition, have a plentiful supply of buns, catchup, mustard, pickle relish, lettuce and sliced cheese, onions and tomatoes.

For *each lb. of meat,* add *1 tsp. salt, 1/4 tsp. pepper, 2 tsp. Worcestershire sauce* and *1 Tbsp. minced onion,* if desired. Mix well; then shape meat into patties. Broil the hamburgers in a preheated broiler, 3 inches from the heat, about 8 minutes, turning once. For cheeseburgers, top with a slice of cheese and broil a minute longer or until cheese melts.

Sloppy Joes

1 Tbsp. butter or margarine	1 tsp. salt
1 lb. ground round steak	1/8 tsp. black pepper
1 cup chopped onion	1 can (10½ oz.) condensed
1 cup chopped celery	tomato soup
1 cup chopped green pepper	1 to 2 tsp. barbecue sauce

Melt butter in a skillet. Add meat; brown it, stirring occasionally and breaking it up into pieces as it cooks. Add remaining ingredients. Continue to cook over low heat, stirring occasionally, 20 to 25 minutes or until vegetables are tender. Spoon into buttered buns. Makes 8 to 10 servings.

SLUMBER PARTY SANDWICHES

Combine *2 cups grated American cheese, 1/2 cup ground peanuts, 2 Tbsp. diced canned pimiento, 2 Tbsp. sweet pickle relish* and enough *salad dressing or mayonnaise* to make mixture spread easily. Spread on *white or whole wheat bread*. Makes about 6 sandwiches.

Boston Beanburgers

6 slices bread, toasted
1 can (1 lb.) baked beans
1/4 cup pickle relish

1 Tbsp. prepared mustard
6 slices processed
  American cheese

Put toast on a baking sheet. Combine beans, relish and mustard; heat well. Pile mixture on toast; top each with a slice of cheese. Place in a broiler 4 inches from heat until cheese browns. Makes 6 servings.

"Morning After" Eggs

Butter a ramekin or shirred egg dish for each serving; pour *1 Tbsp. heavy cream* into each. Break *2 eggs* into each ramekin; sprinkle with *salt, pepper,* and *paprika*. Dot with *butter*. Arrange ramekins in shallow pan; bake in a moderate oven, 350°, 12 to 18 minutes, or until eggs are set.

AFTER-THE-GAME SUPPER
Pizza Pie*
Celery   Carrot Sticks
Pickles and Olives
Ice Cream   Cake
Milk   Carbonated Drinks
*Recipe below.

PIZZA PIE

1 pkg. hot roll mix
3 Tbsp. olive oil
1 can (6 oz.) tomato paste
1/2 cup water

1/4 tsp. salt
1/8 tsp. pepper
1/2 tsp. oregano
1 can (4 oz.) anchovy fillets
1/2 lb. mozzarella cheese, sliced thin

Prepare hot roll mix as directed on package. Let dough rise once. Set oven for hot, 400°. Turn dough out on a lightly floured board. Roll dough until large enough to cover a greased pizza pan 18 inches in diameter. Place dough in pan. Turn under edge to make a 1/4-inch rim. Brush with a little of the olive oil. Combine tomato paste, water, salt, pepper and oregano and spread over the dough. Arrange anchovies and cheese on top; sprinkle remaining olive oil over the top. Bake about 20 minutes or until dough browns and cheese melts. Makes 6 servings.

PIZZA A LA ANDY: Combine *1/2 cup minced sautéed onion, 1/2 cup minced sautéed green pepper* and *3/4 cup chopped Italian sausage.* Prepare 1 recipe Pizza Pie, above, but substitute the onion mixture for the anchovy fillets. Bake as directed above.

87

JELLY ROLL DIPLOMAS

Use the recipe for Festive Ice Cream Roll (see page 29), making the following changes: Grease and line with waxed paper two 15 x 10 x 1-inch pans. Sift a little confectioners' sugar over 4 tea towels. Prepare 1 recipe of cake batter as directed, but divide it between the 2 pans. Bake in a hot oven, 400°, about 9 minutes.

When baked, quickly handle each cake as follows: Invert cake on a towel and remove pan. Peel off paper. Trim crisp edges with a sharp knife; cut cake in half, lengthwise. Put each half cake on a towel. Starting from the long side, roll up each half in towel. Cool on a rack. Unroll cakes, one at a time, remove towel and spread cake at once with currant jelly. Reroll immediately and cut each roll crosswise into 5 equal lengths. Tie each roll with ribbon to make a diploma. Makes 20 rolls.

FOODARAMA FREEZING TIP: Jelly Roll Diplomas may be made ahead of time, then wrapped and stored in the Freezing Compartment of your Foodarama until needed. Tie with ribbons on the day of the party.

HALLOWE'EN MAGIC

Who can resist the time of the black cats and full moon, grinning Jack-O-Lanterns and cherubic Trick or Treaters? Hallowe'en for young and old and in-betweeners is party time. Atmosphere galore awaits your guests.

They arrive at a well-lighted house (on the outside), but the front door opens and they step into darkness. The host shakes hands (using a rubber glove filled with crushed ice). A chill wind (a bowl of ice cubes in front of a fan) and the sound of clanking chains and clacking bones, moans and groans, greet them. They are led through a maze of spider webs (wet strips of cloth dangling from the ceiling; toy spiders and bats (suspended by threads) flutter overhead; a row of horribly grinning faces suddenly come alive (dime store masks placed over Christmas tree lights).

If the guests survive, the lights go on and more Hallowe'en atmosphere surrounds them — cornstalks, autumn leaves, paper skeletons and witches. The party table white cloth is scattered with little, black paper cut-outs of owls, bats and cats. A great, jolly, lighted Jack-O-Lantern centerpiece rests in a circle of bright red apples, nuts and oranges, and white candles are based in cored red apples. Or sprinkle your white cloth with orange, yellow and red confetti, and use small, hollowed-out pumpkins as "containers" (lined with aluminum foil) for spoons, napkins, sugar, favors, candles, etc.

A contrasting centerpiece might be a decorative basket filled with autumn leaves, or apples, nuts and grapes. Serve cider in a jug or a wooden bucket and doughnuts "on a stick" (one or two sawed-down broom handles, nailed to wood board bases).

Children love "Black Cat" favors made of black gumdrops held together by toothpicks.

Fortunes must be told, apples bobbed for; add Musical Chairs, a corn candy Treasure Hunt and Charades.

MULLED CIDER

Combine *1 qt. apple cider, 1/4 cup firmly packed brown sugar, 6 whole cloves and 2 (2 in. ea.) cinnamon sticks* in a saucepan. Bring to a boil; simmer 5 minutes. Strain. Serve hot in mugs or cups. Makes 6 servings.

Old-Fashioned Doughnuts

4½ cups sifted all-purpose flour	1/4 cup shortening
4 tsp. baking powder	1 cup sugar
1/4 tsp. nutmeg	2 eggs
1/2 tsp. salt	1 cup milk
	Fat or cooking oil

Sift together flour and next 3 ingredients. Cream shortening; add and blend in sugar a little at a time. Add eggs, one at a time, blending well after each addition. Add milk and sifted dry ingredients alternately; stir just until well blended after each addition. Chill in the Fresh Food Compartment of your Foodarama about 1/2 hour.

Roll out dough, about 1/4 inch thick, on a lightly floured board. Cut out doughnuts using a floured doughnut cutter.

Melt fat or pour cooking oil into a deep fat fryer or kettle to a depth of 3 to 4 inches; heat to 375°. Fry doughnuts until brown, about 3 minutes; turn once. Drain on absorbent paper. Serve plain, or sprinkle with confectioners' sugar, if desired. Makes about 24 doughnuts.

TRICK OR TREAT COOKIES

4 cups sifted all-purpose flour
2 tsp. cinnamon
1 tsp. salt
1/4 tsp. baking soda
1 cup plus 2 Tbsp. firmly packed
  brown sugar

1 cup butter or margarine
1 cup molasses
1/2 tsp. vinegar
Confectioners' Icing—white, orange,
  red and green (see page 33)

Sift together the flour, cinnamon, salt and baking soda into a medium-size bowl. Mix in sugar. Cut in butter with pastry blender or 2 knives until mixture resembles coarse corn meal. Add molasses and vinegar; stir until thoroughly blended. Cover bowl; chill dough in the Fresh Food Compartment of your Foodarama until very firm or about 3 to 4 hours.

Set oven for moderate, 350°. Grease and flour cooky sheets.

On a lightly floured board, roll out chilled dough, a little at a time, about 1/8 inch thick. Cut dough with floured cooky cutters in shapes of witches, cats and pumpkins; place on cooky sheets. Bake 8 to 10 minutes, or until edges of cookies are slightly crisp. Remove from sheets and cool cookies on a wire rack. Decorate, as shown, with icing, using a pastry tube or wooden pick for drawing lines. Makes about 10 to 12 dozen cookies depending on the size of the cutters.

APPLESAUCE LOAF

1¾ cups sifted all-purpose flour
1½ tsp. cinnamon
1 tsp. allspice
1 tsp. nutmeg
1/4 tsp. ground cloves

1/2 tsp. salt
1 tsp. baking soda
1/2 cup shortening
1 cup sugar
1 egg, well beaten
1 cup unsweetened applesauce

Set oven for moderate, 350°. Grease a loaf pan, about 9 x 5 x 3 inches. Sift together flour and next 6 ingredients; set aside.

Cream shortening in a mixing bowl. Slowly add and beat in sugar; beat until well blended. Add and beat in egg. Add and stir in applesauce. Add sifted dry ingredients, stirring only enough to blend. Turn cake batter into pan. Bake 50 to 60 minutes. Cool cake slightly in pan on a wire rack. Remove from pan; cool on rack. Frost with Butter Frosting, if desired.

BUTTER FROSTING

Blend *2 cups sifted confectioners' sugar* with *1/4 cup butter or margarine.* Gradually add about *2 Tbsp. cream.* Stir until smooth. Add *1/2 tsp. vanilla, 1/2 tsp. orange extract* and *a few drops each yellow and red food coloring,* if desired. Stir to blend.

A THANKSGIVING FEAST

A treasure of a family holiday, full of warm-hearted moments and gustatory delights savored long after the turkey bones are bare, the Thanksgiving Day party quite naturally centers around the groaning board. If you're a hostess who really enjoys her own parties, then practically everything has been prepared in advance.

Your house is organized for a crowd, and full of festive touches: corner baskets or jugs of cornstalks and winter grasses, vases of bright autumn flowers and leaves, baskets and bowls looking like still-life paintings with their handsome arrays of fruits and nuts and Indian corn. The Thanksgiving table is set with your prettiest cloth and appointments. The ever-perfect centerpiece is that traditional symbol of a plentiful harvest: red cabbage, acorn and yellow squash, white and yellow onions, pumpkin, eggplant, green peppers, apples, grapes and oranges—all arranged on a tray lined with autumn leaves. Tall yellow candles in your prettiest glass holders flank the centerpiece. Or, if the table is long, try twin end centerpieces made of two small, hollowed-out pumpkins filled with vivid autumn flowers.

Many hostesses prefer the junior members of the family — interruptions, spilled milk and all — to be seated at the table with the adults. Others like to set a second, smaller table for the small-fry. If this is your preference, duplicate on a smaller scale, the main table's decorations. Or the children's table might have a centerpiece tray of chocolate turkeys, roosting in a bed of autumn leaves. Around each bird's neck is a yellow ribbon leading out to each place setting.

Simple family games for after dinner include Nut Throw (take turns pitching unshelled nuts into a bowl set a few feet away), Thanksgiving Day (make words from the letters in "Thanksgiving Day"), Nut Relay (push a nut along the floor over the finish line — but push only with the nose!).

93

THANKSGIVING DINNER
Roast Turkey with Oyster Stuffing*
Orange Glazed Yams*
Wax Beans and Mushrooms*
Creamed Onions with
Buttered Almonds*
Cranberry Sauce*   Relishes   Corn Sticks
Grandma's Pumpkin Pie*
Coffee

*Recipes on pages 96-100.

ROAST TURKEY WITH OYSTER STUFFING

(see pic., page 94)

Select a plump, ready-to-cook turkey. Allow 1/2 to 3/4 pound per serving and buy a turkey large enough for seconds and leftovers.

PREPARATION FOR ROASTING: Allow sufficient time to thaw the turkey if it is frozen, and use it within 24 hours after it is thawed. Remove any pinfeathers with tweezers or catch them between thumb and paring knife. Remove bits of lung and liver and any large layers of fat. Wash bird inside and out under cold running water; drain well and dry with paper towels. Wrap loosely in waxed paper; chill in the Fresh Food Compartment of your Foodarama until ready to stuff.

STUFFING AND TRUSSING: Rub body cavity lightly with salt. Spoon stuffing into cavity; do not pack. Allow about 1 cup stuffing per pound. (Leftover stuffing may be placed in a casserole and baked separately; spoon pan drippings over stuffing in the casserole occasionally, if desired.) To close cavity, insert wooden picks or metal skewers along edges of the skin; lace with twine. Fill neck cavity loosely and skewer neck skin to the back. Tie legs together and fasten to tail. Fold wings under turkey or tie wings to body. Roast at once.

ROASTING THE TURKEY: Rub skin of turkey generously with melted shortening. Place bird, breast side up, on a rack in a shallow pan or open roaster. Insert a meat thermometer in thickest part of thigh, close to body. Cover bird with a double thickness of cheese cloth dipped in melted shortening. Roast in a moderately low oven, 325°. Baste often with pan drippings or shortening. Remove cloth during last hour of roasting. Bird is done when meat on leg can be easily pierced with a fork; thermometer should register 190°.

Allow 3 to 4 hours for 4 to 8-lb. birds; 4 to 4½ hours for 8 to 12-lb. birds; 4½ to 5 hours for 12 to 16-lb. birds; 5½ to 7 hours for 16 to 20-lb. birds; 7 to 8 hours for 20 to 24-lb. birds.

Oyster Stuffing

4 cups diced celery	1 Tbsp. salt
1½ cups boiling salted water	1 tsp. pepper
1/2 cup chopped onion	4 qt. (16 cups) day-old bread cubes
3/4 cup butter or margarine	1½ cups fresh or frozen raw oysters
2 tsp. poultry seasoning	with oyster liquor

Put celery and salted water in a pan; cook, covered, until tender. Drain; reserve 1 cup of the liquid. Cook onions in butter until tender; add celery. In a large bowl, combine seasonings, bread cubes, celery mixture and reserved celery liquid. Chop oysters and add with their liquor to the bread mixture. Mix well. If a more moist stuffing is desired, add 1/2 cup hot water and stir well. Makes enough to stuff a 16-lb. turkey.

ORANGE GLAZED YAMS
(see pic., page 94)

8 medium-size cooked yams
    or sweet potatoes,
    cut in halves
	1 can thawed, frozen orange juice
	    concentrate, undiluted
	1/4 cup butter or margarine

Arrange yams in a single layer in a baking dish. Brush generously with orange juice concentrate; dot with butter. Bake in a hot oven, 400°, about 20 minutes, brushing frequently with juice and pan drippings until yams are well-glazed and golden brown. Makes 8 servings.

WAX BEANS AND MUSHROOMS
(see pic., page 94)

4 Tbsp. butter or margarine 1 small onion, chopped 1/2 lb. mushrooms, thinly sliced	2 pkg. (about 10 oz. ea.) frozen wax beans, cooked and drained Salt and pepper

Melt butter in a skillet; add onion and mushrooms; cook until lightly browned. Add wax beans and salt and pepper to taste; toss gently. Cover and simmer 3 to 4 minutes to heat well. Makes 8 servings.

CORN, HARVEST STYLE

Cook *2 pkg. (about 10 oz. ea.) frozen whole-kernel corn* according to package directions; drain. Melt *6 Tbsp. butter or margarine* in a skillet. Add *1/2 cup chopped green pepper* and *1/2 cup chopped red pepper or pimiento*. Cook, covered, over low heat 3 minutes or until tender. Add corn and *salt and pepper* to taste. Stir and heat well. Makes 8 servings.

CREAMED ONIONS
WITH BUTTERED ALMONDS
(see pic., page 94)

2½ lb. white onions, cooked
3 cups Medium White Sauce
  (see recipe below)

1 cup blanched slivered almonds
2 Tbsp. butter or margarine
Salt, pepper and paprika

Add onions to white sauce; heat gently. Brown almonds in hot butter in a small skillet; add seasonings to taste. To serve, mix half the almonds into creamed onions. Turn into serving dish or casserole; sprinkle with remaining almonds. Makes 8 servings.

MEDIUM WHITE SAUCE: Melt *4 Tbsp. butter or margarine* in a saucepan. Remove from heat; blend in *4 Tbsp. flour, 1 tsp. salt, 1/4 tsp. pepper;* slowly stir in *2 cups milk.* Cook over medium heat 5 to 8 minutes; stir constantly until thick and smooth. Makes about 2 cups sauce.

Broccoli California

2 pkg. (about 10 oz. ea.) frozen
  broccoli
1/3 cup olive oil or butter
1 clove garlic, crushed

1/4 cup chopped almonds, if desired
2/3 cup sliced, pitted ripe olives
2 tsp. lemon juice

Cook broccoli according to package directions. Drain and keep warm. Put olive oil and garlic in a small saucepan. Place over medium heat; cook 2 minutes, stirring occasionally. Add nuts, olives and lemon juice; heat thoroughly. Sprinkle over the broccoli. Makes 6 to 8 servings.

Three Layer Salad

2 pkg. (3 oz. ea.) lemon-
flavored gelatin
2 cups boiling water
2 cups cold water
2/3 cup chopped sweet pickle

2/3 cup chopped walnuts
2/3 cup sliced stuffed
olives
Curly endive
Lemon Cups (see recipe below)

Empty gelatin into a bowl and dissolve it in the boiling water; stir in cold
water. Add and stir in pickles, nuts and olives. Pour into a 6-cup mold;
chill in the Fresh Food Compartment of your Foodarama until firm.
(Pickles, nuts and olives will self-layer.) Unmold on a platter. Garnish
salad with endive and Lemon Cups. Makes 8 to 12 servings.

LEMON CUPS: Remove blossom ends from lemons; cut lemons in half
crosswise. Squeeze out juice. Remove membrane from the peel using a
teaspoon. Dip cut edges of peel in paprika. Fill cups with mayonnaise.

CRANBERRY SAUCE

Wash and pick over *4 cups (1 lb.) cranberries*. Combine *2 cups sugar* and
2 cups boiling water in a saucepan; stir until sugar dissolves. Boil 5 minutes; add berries and boil without stirring until all berries pop open. Chill
in the Fresh Food Compartment of your Foodarama before serving.
Makes about 1 quart.

BANANAS MELBA

1 pkg. (10 oz.) frozen raspberries
6 firm bananas
2 Tbsp. lemon juice

Sugar
1/4 cup butter or margarine
1/2 cup toasted shredded coconut

Thaw the raspberries. Peel bananas; brush with lemon juice and roll in sugar to coat well. Melt butter in a large skillet. Add bananas and fry slowly over medium heat until fork-tender and golden, turning to brown evenly. Roll bananas in coconut and immediately arrange on a serving dish. Spoon part of the raspberries over the bananas and serve with remaining berries on the side. Makes 6 servings.

GRANDMA'S PUMPKIN PIE

(see pic., page 94)

1 can (1 lb. 13 oz.) or 3½ cups
   cooked pumpkin
1 cup brown sugar
1 cup white sugar
1/4 tsp. cloves
3 tsp. cinnamon
2 tsp. ginger
1/4 tsp. nutmeg

1 tsp. salt
4 eggs, beaten
1 cup evaporated milk
1 cup heavy cream
2 unbaked 9-inch pastry shells
   (see recipe on page 28)
Sweetened whipped cream
Diced preserved or candied ginger

Set oven for moderate, 350°. Combine pumpkin, sugars and spices in a large bowl; mix well. Mix in salt and eggs. Combine milk and cream in saucepan; heat to scalding point. Add to pumpkin mixture; stir until blended. Pour into unbaked pastry shells. Bake about 1 hour or until a knife inserted near edge comes out clean. At serving time, make a border of whipped cream around the edges; sprinkle with ginger. Makes 2 pies.

NOTE: For 1 large pie, fit pastry into a deep 10-inch pie pan; fill with above pumpkin mixture and bake 1½ hours.

Pumpkin Pecan Pie

Prepare Pumpkin Pie as above, and start to bake.

For each pie, blend together *1 Tbsp. butter, 2 Tbsp. brown sugar,* and *1 Tbsp. grated orange peel;* mix in *3/4 cup whole pecans.* About 10 minutes before pies finish baking, sprinkle sugar-nut mixture over the filling. Then return pies to oven for remaining baking time. Topping will glaze pies.

ORANGE MINCE PIE

1 pkg. (9 oz.)
  condensed mincemeat
3/4 cup water

1 can (6 oz.) frozen orange
  juice concentrate, thawed
Pastry (see recipe on page 28)

Put mincemeat in a saucepan and break into small pieces with a spoon. Add and stir in water and orange juice. Cook and stir over high heat until lumps are broken. Boil 1 minute; remove from heat and set aside to cool.

On a lightly floured board roll out half the pastry into an 11-inch circle. Line an 8-inch pie pan with pastry. Turn mincemeat into pastry-lined pan. Complete pie either as a lattice top as pictured, or as a 2-crust pie. Bake in a hot oven, 425°, 30 minutes or until golden.

POKER for the MEN

These parties need no frills. Have ready in advance: hearty, appetizing foods in oven casseroles or platters of cold cuts; coffee measured, waiting to be made. This guarantees ease for the host; pleasure for his guests.

PAELLA

18 cherrystone clams, well-scrubbed	Salt and pepper
1 ready-to-cook chicken, 2½ lb., cut up	1 can (11 oz.) condensed chicken consommé
Seasoned flour	2 large green peppers, diced
3 Tbsp. fat	4 medium-size onions, chopped
Water	3 cloves garlic, peeled
1 lb. sweet Spanish sausages	1½ cups cooked peas
1 cup rice	1 can (20 oz.) chick-peas
1/2 to 1 tsp. saffron	2 lb. shrimp, cooked and cleaned

Soak clams in cold, salted water to remove sand. Dredge chicken in seasoned flour. Brown chicken evenly in fat. Add 1/2 cup water; simmer, covered, 25 minutes or until tender. Cut sausages in 1-inch pieces and brown; drain, saving sausage fat. Put 2 tablespoons of the fat in skillet.

Add rice; sprinkle with saffron, salt and pepper. Cook until rice is transparent. Mix consommé with 4 cups water; stir into rice. Cook until rice is tender. Heat more fat in skillet. Add peppers, onion and garlic; cook until tender. Discard garlic. Combine rice, pepper mixture, sausage, peas and chick-peas. Alternate layers of rice mixture, chicken, shrimp and 12 clams in a 3-quart casserole. Half bury remaining clams on top. Bake in a moderately low oven, 325°, 15 minutes, until hot. Makes 8 to 12 servings.

CRUNCHY NIBBLERS

4 cups bite-size shredded rice biscuits	1 can salted peanuts
4 cups bite-size shredded wheat biscuits	1/2 lb. butter or margarine, melted
4 cups ready-to-eat oat cereal	2 Tbsp. Worcestershire sauce
1 small box pretzel sticks	2 tsp. celery salt
	1 tsp. garlic salt
	2 tsp. seasoned salt

Mix cereals, pretzels and nuts in a baking pan. Combine rest of ingredients; pour over the mixture. Heat in low oven, 250°, 1 hour; stir often.

SAUSAGE PLATTER

Select several kinds of sliced sausage such as bologna, pressed ham and olive loaf. Arrange some slices on the platter, as pictured. Make roll-ups of the remaining slices: Spread each slice with a little prepared mustard and wrap around strips of cheese, dill pickle, or water cress.

Christmas, the most beloved, the gayest holiday of all is anticipated for weeks, enjoyed through each precious day of the Holiday Season, and remembered with nostalgia right up until it's time, once more, to set out the holly and mistletoe. Christmastime, children say, is having a party every day! Invite guests to your special gathering with a Christmas tree or ornament-design invitation decorated with stars and glitter. (See INVITATIONS, Page 6.)

The holiday atmosphere begins right at the front door with a cheerful, inviting decoration: a bouquet of evergreens wearing a huge red bow and non-breakable ornaments, and a porch jug full of similarly decorated branches. Or make a Christmas tree frontispiece. Force a coat-hanger wire into a tree shape; cover with chicken wire, allowing an extra half-inch for a fold-over edge. Fill the holes with little evergreen branches to cover, and decorate with miniature ornaments. Hang a leather strap or red ribbon of jingle bells to tinkle a welcome as the door is opened.

Inside, a miniature Sugarplum Tree stands on a table near the door. Candy canes, cookies or paper-wrapped candies (held on by ornament hooks) hang from its branches, and each child guest is treated to the sugarplums. Christmas cards may decorate another table-tree, or a wall, or form a frame around the fireplace.

Your mantle is aglow with tall, handsome candles nested in evergreens or holly. A sideboard display of decorative candles, in interesting antique bottle "candleholders," adds an original note. Baskets and bowls of fruit and cookies have festive touches of evergreens and red ribbon bows.

An archway or large window takes on a modern holiday mood when filled with a row of round ornaments, hung two inches apart and at varying heights. For another type of "mobile," use a white styrofoam "snowball" as a base. Stick the ends of small evergreen branches into the ball until it is completely covered, then decorate the branches with tiny ornaments.

Suspend the balls from ceiling fixtures, or suspend several over the buffet

table as a canopy. The inexpensive, colorful aluminum foil ornaments also make charming canopies.

The party table is highlighted by your lovely Christmas foods. As background, try a red cloth runner, or a white cloth crisscrossed by wide red ribbons. A single massive red candle (or three white candles of different heights), based in holly, rests on the ribbon crossing. Or what could be prettier than a large milk-glass centerpiece bowl filled with white-sprayed evergreen branches and trimmed with little white ornaments, or a silver bowl filled with silver balls and holly leaves? A whimsical "Christmas tree" centerpiece is made by combining pieces of driftwood into an abstract tree shape, trimmed with the most traditional of decorations: strings of popcorn and cranberries, gingerbread men, miniature candles, etc. Between the dishes of food, little arrangements of cotton-glitter "snow" or "angel hair" hold delicate Christmas figurines, a pair of your prettiest ornaments, a pair of painted pine cones dipped in glitter. Tinsel or ropes of miniature ornaments may be wound around and about the dishes. Each main dish may be highlighted by a candle placed at its side: base the candle in a styrofoam "snowball" sprinkled with sequins or glitter, or in a shiny, red, cored apple.

For the children, make delightful fat snowman favors: a popcorn ball for the body, a smaller one for the head, gumdrop feet and features, and a lollipop "broom." For adult favors, charming little corsages and boutonnieres are easily made by wiring together a cluster of holly leaves and two or three tiny ornaments; tie with a red or green ribbon and attach a safety pin onto the back.

Don't forget to sing your favorite carols and to read aloud the endearing classic Christmas stories. For Christmas games, play "Living Christmas Trees." Each team selects one member to be decorated as the "tree." Use green crepe paper, unbreakable ornaments, aluminum-foil paper, tinsel, pins, needle and thread, scissors and paste. Judge the masterpieces, and award prizes. See Party Games on pages 12 and 13 for other games to play. Adapt games such as Treasure Hunt to your Christmas theme.

SPRINGERLE

4½ cups sifted cake flour	3½ cups (1 lb.) sifted confectioners' sugar
1 tsp. baking powder	Grated peel of 1½ lemons
4 eggs	2 Tbsp. anise seeds

Sift together flour and baking powder. Return to sifter. Beat eggs until lemon-colored. Slowly add and stir in sugar and grated peel; beat to blend well. Sift flour mixture, a little at a time, over egg mixture; stir to blend well. Dough will be stiff. Cover dough; chill in the Fresh Food Compartment of your Foodarama. Grease cooky sheets; sprinkle with anise seeds. On a lightly floured board, roll out dough, into 1/4-inch thick rectangles. Flour springerle rolling pin well and roll over dough, pressing down just enough to leave clear-cut designs; sprinkle rolling pin with flour as needed. Use a floured, sharp, long-bladed knife to cut cookies apart. Put cookies on sheets. Let stand, uncovered, at least 12 hours to set design and dry tops.

Set oven for moderate, 350°. Bake cookies 10 minutes, or until very pale brown. Remove from cooky sheets; cool on a wire rack. Store in an airtight container 2 to 3 weeks to develop flavor. These cookies are very crisp—almost hard—with a delicate anise flavor. Makes about 4½ dozen.

SANTA CLAUS COOKIES

4 cups sifted all-purpose flour
1/2 tsp. baking soda
1/4 tsp. salt
1 cup butter or margarine
2 cups sugar
3 eggs

1 tsp. vanilla
Red and White Confectioners' Icing
  (see page 33)
Red cinnamon candies
Shredded coconut
Green sugar

Sift together flour, baking soda and salt. Cream butter; slowly add and beat in sugar and continue beating until well blended. Add eggs, one at a time, beating well after each addition; blend in vanilla. Add sifted dry ingredients gradually; blend well. Cover bowl; chill dough in the Fresh Food Compartment of your Foodarama several hours or until firm enough to roll.

Set oven for moderate, 350°. Grease cooky sheets. On a lightly floured board, roll out chilled dough, 1/4 inch thick. Cut with floured Santa Claus cooky cutter; place on cooky sheets. Bake 8 to 10 minutes, or until cookies are golden. Run spatula under cookies to remove from sheets. Cool on wire racks. Decorate as shown with icing, candies, coconut and sugar. Makes about 4 dozen.

FOODARAMA FREEZING TIP: Make Santa Claus Cookies and Springerle (see page 106) in the fall when you have plenty of time, and freeze them in the Freezing Compartment of your Foodarama until the holidays.

BRAZIL NUT CAKE

1½ cups shelled, whole Brazil nuts
1 lb. pitted dates
1 cup maraschino cherries, drained
3/4 cup sifted all-purpose flour

3/4 cup sugar
1/2 tsp. baking powder
1/2 tsp. salt
3 eggs
1 tsp. vanilla

Set oven for slow, 300°. Grease a 9 x 5 x 3-inch loaf pan and line with waxed paper.

Combine nuts, dates and cherries in a large bowl. Sift together flour, sugar, baking powder and salt and add to nut-fruit mixture. Mix well to coat nuts and fruit and distribute flour evenly.

Beat eggs until foamy; beat in vanilla. Add to nut-fruit mixture and stir until well mixed. Turn into prepared pan and spread evenly. Bake 1 hour and 45 minutes. Cool cake in pan about 10 to 15 minutes on a rack. Remove from pan; peel off waxed paper at once and let cake stand on a rack until cool. Chill in the Fresh Food Compartment of your Foodarama before slicing. Makes one 3-pound cake.

Berliner Kranser
(see pic. at right)

3/4 cup shortening
3/4 cup butter
1 cup sugar
2 eggs
2 tsp. grated orange peel
3¾ cups sifted all-purpose flour

1 egg white
Red and green sugar
Red cinnamon candies
Citron, cut in strips
Red candied cherries,
    cut in quarters

Cream shortening, butter and sugar together; beat until well blended. Add eggs, one at a time; beat well after each addition. Stir in orange peel. Add flour, a little at a time; stir until well blended; chill in the Fresh Food Compartment of your Foodarama.

Set oven for hot, 400°. On a lightly floured board, roll out dough 1/4 inch thick and cut with doughnut cutter. Place on ungreased cooky sheets. Brush tops with egg white. Decorate with red and green sugar, candies, citron and cherries. Bake 10 to 12 minutes. Remove from sheet; cool on a wire rack. Makes about 6 dozen.

Christmas Punch

1 cup sugar
1 cup water
4 cups bottled cranberry juice
1½ cups lemon juice

2 cups orange juice
2 cups unsweetened pineapple juice
Block of ice or
    Della Robbia Ice Ring
2 bot. (28 oz. ea.) ginger ale

Combine sugar and water in a small saucepan. Bring to boil, stirring until sugar dissolves. Cover and boil over low heat, without stirring, for about

5 minutes. Combine the sugar syrup and all the fruit juices. Chill thoroughly in the Fresh Food Compartment of your Foodarama.

Just before serving time, put a block of ice or a Della Robbia Ice Ring in a punch bowl. Pour in fruit juice mixture. Ladle punch over the ice until well chilled. Pour in the ginger ale. Makes 24 to 30 punch-cup servings.

DELLA ROBBIA ICE RING

You need a ring mold or an angel food cake pan and a variety of small fruits such as cherries, small bunches of grapes, kumquats, strawberries, raspberries, cranberries, lady apples, small limes, apricots, plums. In addition it's a good idea to have some laurel, mint, holly or lemon leaves. Wash fruit and leaves well.

Arrange a layer of fruit and leaves, top side down, in the mold. Pour in ice water to a depth of 3/4 inch. Some of the fruit will not be covered with water. Put the pan in the Freezing Compartment of the Foodarama until water is frozen. Quickly arrange another layer of fruit and pour in another layer of ice water. Freeze. Repeat until mold is filled. To use, unmold and put bottom side up, in the bowl of punch.

CHRISTMAS GOOSE

When buying a goose for roasting, allow about 1 pound "ready-to-cook" weight per serving. Goose varies in "ready-to-cook" weight from 4 to 14 pounds. If frozen, allow time for thawing.

To prepare and stuff the goose, follow directions given for turkey on page 96. Use Nut and Fruit Stuffing below or your own favorite recipe. Insert a meat thermometer so tip rests in center of stuffing. Roast in a moderately low oven, 325°. Place bird, breast side down, on a rack in a shallow pan or open roaster. When 2/3 done, turn bird breast side up; finish roasting.

Goose should be cooked until well done, 185°, on a meat thermometer. For a bird 4 to 8 lb., allow 2¾ to 3½ hrs.; 8 to 12 lb., 3½ to 4½ hrs.; 12 to 14 lb., about 4¾ hrs.

Nut and Fruit Stuffing

2 pkg. (8 oz. ea.) bread stuffing
3 ripe bananas, mashed
1 cup halved, seeded Tokay grapes

2 tart apples, pared, cored and diced
2 oranges, sectioned
1 cup broken walnut meats

Prepare bread stuffing as directed on package. Blend in bananas. Add remaining ingredients; mix well. Makes about 3½ quarts, enough for a 14-pound goose.

Holiday Orange Pudding

3 cups soft, coarse bread crumbs
1 cup warm milk
1/2 cup melted butter or margarine
1 cup sweet orange marmalade
1 cup sifted all-purpose flour
1 tsp. baking soda

1 tsp. salt
1/4 tsp. nutmeg
1/4 tsp. cloves
1/4 tsp. cinnamon
1 cup mixed, diced candied
    fruits and peels

Place a rack in bottom of a steamer or kettle. Pour in water just to top of rack. Grease a 1-qt. mold. Just before mixing pudding, cover steamer and bring water to boiling.

Place bread crumbs in a bowl. Add milk, butter and marmalade; blend well. Sift together flour and next 5 ingredients; stir into crumb mixture. Add fruits and peels; stir to mix well. Turn into mold; cover tightly. Place mold on a rack in steamer. Cover and steam pudding 3 hours; add water as needed. Cool pudding on a wire rack 5 minutes; unmold and serve warm. Decorate platter with Hard Sauce Snowmen, if desired. Makes 8 servings.

HARD SAUCE SNOWMEN: Beat *2/3 cup butter or margarine* until creamy. Blend in *3 cups sifted confectioners' sugar*. Chill in the Fresh Food Compartment of your Foodarama. Shape into 1½-inch balls for bodies, 3/4-inch balls for heads and 1/2-inch balls for feet. Assemble, as shown. Use *cloves* and *bits of candied cherries* for eyes and mouth, *cinnamon candies* for buttons, *candied cherry halves* for hats.

CHRISTMAS EVE BUFFET

Creamed Diced Ham, Oysters
and Mushrooms*
Browned Rice*   Hot Biscuits*
Mustard Salad Molds*
Glazed Cranberry Pie*
Coffee

Recipes on pages 114 and 115.

CREAMED HAM, OYSTERS AND MUSHROOMS

(see pic., page 112)

1 pt. fresh or frozen shucked oysters with liquor (about 24)	1 cup butter or margarine
5 cups light cream, about	3/4 cup flour
1 lb. fresh mushrooms	Salt and pepper
	1 lb. (2½ cups) cooked diced ham

Cook oysters gently in their own liquor until edges curl. Drain the oysters; set aside. Measure the oyster liquor; add enough cream to make 6 cups.

Wash mushrooms; slice or cut in halves if mushrooms are large. Cook them in 1/4 cup of the butter until golden brown and tender; set aside. Melt remaining 3/4 cup butter in a large saucepan over medium heat. Remove from heat. Blend in flour, salt and pepper to taste; mix well. Slowly add and stir in cream mixture. Return to medium heat. Cook 5 to 8 minutes, stirring constantly until thick and smooth. Add oysters, mushrooms and ham; heat well. Makes 8 to 10 servings.

BROWNED RICE

Melt *1/2 cup butter or margarine* in a large heavy saucepan over low heat. Add *2 cups drained washed rice.* Cook, stirring frequently, until rice is yellow. Dissolve *6 chicken bouillon cubes* and *1 tsp. salt* in *8 cups boiling water;* slowly add to rice. Cover and simmer without stirring about 25 minutes, or until rice is tender, dry and flaky. Makes 8 to 10 servings.

Hot Herb Biscuits

2½ cups sifted all-purpose flour
4 tsp. baking powder
1/2 tsp. curry powder
1/2 tsp. ground basil leaves
1/2 tsp. salt
1/3 cup shortening or butter
2 Tbsp. minced parsley
1/2 tsp. dried celery leaves, crumbled
3/4 cup milk, about

Set oven for very hot, 450°. Sift together flour, baking powder, curry powder, basil and salt. Add and cut in shortening, parsley and celery. Add and stir in just enough milk to make a soft dough. Turn out on a lightly floured board. Knead gently 15 to 20 turns. Roll or pat out dough 1/2 inch thick. Then cut out 2-inch rounds using a floured cutter. Arrange on ungreased cooky sheets. Bake 12 to 15 minutes or until brown. Makes about 16 biscuits.

BAKING POWDER BISCUITS: Follow directions for Herb Biscuits above, omitting the curry powder, basil, parsley and celery.

Mustard Salad Molds
(see pic., page 112)

1 envel. unflavored gelatin	3 eggs, slightly beaten
1/4 cup cold water	1/2 cup finely diced celery
3/4 cup sugar	1 cup cooked green peas
1 Tbsp. dry mustard	1/2 cup diced canned pimiento
3/4 tsp. salt	Watercress or other crisp
1 cup vinegar	salad greens

Soften gelatin in cold water. In the top of a double boiler, combine sugar, mustard, salt. Stir in vinegar and eggs. Cook and stir over hot water until thickened. Remove from heat. Add the softened gelatin; stir until dissolved. Set pan in a bowl of ice water, stirring occasionally, until slightly thickened; fold in celery, peas and pimiento. Turn into 8 to 10 individual molds. Chill in the Fresh Food Compartment of your Foodarama until set. Unmold on a serving plate. Garnish with watercress. Makes 8 to 10 servings.

Glazed Cranberry Pie
(see pic., page 112)

2 cups sugar	1 Tbsp. grated orange peel
1/2 tsp. cinnamon	2 Tbsp. butter or margarine
1 Tbsp. flour	Pastry for 9-inch pie (see page 28)
1/4 tsp. salt	1 egg white
1/3 cup hot water	1 Tbsp. lemon juice
4 cups fresh or frozen cranberries	1 cup confectioners' sugar

Combine sugar, cinnamon, flour and salt. Pour water into a heavy metal saucepan or large skillet. Add sugar mixture and stir well. Cook over very low heat, stirring constantly, until sugar melts. Add cranberries and stir gently. Continue to cook over low heat until berries pop open. Add and stir in orange peel and butter.

Roll out half the pastry and line a 9-inch pie pan. Roll out remaining pastry and cut in 3/4-inch strips. Pour berries into pastry-lined pan. Use pastry strips to make a lattice top, as shown. Trim edges; press to seal and flute or crimp, as desired.

Combine remaining ingredients. Pour over the pie. Bake in a hot oven, 425°, 30 minutes or until brown.

NEW YEAR'S PARTIES

New Year's Day parties have a most special quality, unlike that of any other party in the year. The atmosphere is gay, yet serene —keyed to the future, yet gently nostalgic—and Open House is the perfect vehicle to carry the day. The emphasis is on the future in this invitation, made from deep blue construction paper (see INVITATIONS, Page 6). A "Satellite in Orbit" dominates the cover (make a white paper circle with black paper antennae, top and bottom, which send off little black paper dots to represent the signal beeps). Silver stars and yellow paper "planets" fill in the galaxy and, inside, your invitation begins, "Come join us in a look at the future, on Saturday . . ."

From there, your imagination takes over. Outer space or life on the moon may set the pace with interesting lighting effects from blue Christmas tree lights behind mists of veiling; a ceiling galaxy of suspended aluminum-foil stars, rocket ships in flight and yellow balloon planets.

Set a pretty table in the living room for the holiday eggnog (tea or coffee is also served). Try a silver bowl centerpiece with silver or blue ornaments. Add tall white candles to complement the centerpiece. Above the table, repeat the futuristic theme: string picture wire overhead, suspend a toy spaceship, tiny silver stars and yellow planets by threads of varying lengths, and have a few "Martians" descending from the spaceship (hang each on a progressively longer string). Make the Martians of round ornaments with painted-on features and taped-on pipe cleaner arms and legs (as many as you think necessary!). Place a few more of your little "other-worlders" on the table, perhaps on their way up the sides of the eggnog bowl.

For your New Year's dinner, spray evergreen branches to match a pretty pink (or any pastel) tablecloth. Trim with pink ornaments and arrange in low silver or glass bowls. Add tall white candles in silver or glass holders and, at each setting, place a single pink carnation in a little bud vase.

116

HOLIDAY EGGNOG

6 eggs, separated	1 pt. chilled milk
1 pt. brandy or whiskey	3/4 cup sugar
1/3 cup dark rum	1 pt. chilled heavy cream, whipped
	Nutmeg

Beat egg yolks until thick. Slowly add and beat in brandy and rum. Stir in milk. Whip egg whites until very foamy. Gradually add and beat in sugar; beat just until egg whites form soft, shiny peaks. Fold egg whites into brandy mixture; fold in cream. Chill in the Fresh Food Compartment of the Foodarama. Serve in a chilled bowl; sprinkle with nutmeg. Makes about 24 servings.

Golden Eggnog

6 eggs, separated	1 Tbsp. vanilla
3/4 cup sugar	1 pt. chilled heavy cream, whipped
1 qt. chilled milk	Nutmeg

Whip egg whites until very foamy. Gradually add and beat in sugar. Beat just until egg whites form soft, shiny peaks. Beat egg yolks until thick. Fold in egg whites. Slowly stir in milk and vanilla. Fold cream into egg mixture. Chill in the Fresh Food Compartment of the Foodarama. Serve in a chilled bowl; sprinkle with nutmeg. Makes about 24 servings.

NEW YEAR'S DAY DINNER

Rib Roast of Beef*

Pan Roasted Potatoes   Squash Supreme*

Green Peas with Water Chestnuts*

Spiced Crabapples

Bavarian Wreath Mold*

Coffee

*Recipes on pages 120 and 121.

RIB ROAST OF BEEF
(see pic., page 118)

Select a 7-inch cut, standing rib roast. Allow 1/2 pound per serving but buy a roast of at least 2 ribs. You must know the weight of a roast in order to estimate cooking time.

Season meat with salt and pepper, if desired. Put roast in a shallow baking pan, fat side up. Roast in a moderately low oven, 325°. Do not cover, add water, or baste.

For the most accurate results, use a meat thermometer. Insert the thermometer so the bulb rests in the thickest part of the meat without touching fat or bone. Thermometer should read 140° for rare, 160° for medium, 170° for well-done, regardless of weight of roast.

For a 3 to 5-lb. roast, allow 26 minutes per lb. for rare; 30 minutes for medium; 35 minutes for well-done. For a 6 to 8-lb. roast, allow 20 minutes per lb. for rare; 25 minutes for medium; 30 minutes for well-done.

Squash Supreme
(see pic., page 118)

8 cups cubed Hubbard or butternut squash	3 Tbsp. brown sugar
Boiling salted water	1/4 cup butter or margarine
1 cup canned crushed pineapple and juice	Dash nutmeg
	1/2 cup cream, about

Cook squash in salted water 15 minutes or until tender. Drain well and mash. Add next 4 ingredients and enough cream to make squash the consistency of mashed potatoes. Heat thoroughly. Makes 8 to 10 servings.

GREEN PEAS WITH WATER CHESTNUTS
(see pic., page 118)

Cook frozen green peas according to package directions. Drain; season with butter, salt and pepper. Combine with sliced, canned water chestnuts. Heat well before serving.

BAVARIAN WREATH MOLD
(see pic., page 118)

2 envel. unflavored gelatin	1 tsp. vanilla
1/4 tsp. salt	1/3 cup sweet sherry
1/2 cup sugar	1 cup heavy cream
3 eggs, separated	Leaf-shaped gumdrops
2¾ cups milk	Red cinnamon candies

Combine gelatin, salt and 1/4 cup of the sugar in the top of a double boiler. Beat egg yolks; stir in milk; slowly stir into gelatin mixture. Place over boiling water; cook and stir until gelatin dissolves and mixture thickens slightly. Remove from heat. Stir in vanilla and sherry. Set pan in a bowl of ice cubes and water. Chill in the Fresh Food Compartment of the Foodarama, stirring often, until mixture mounds slightly when dropped from a spoon.

Whip egg whites until foamy; gradually beat in remaining sugar, beating until stiff. Whip cream; fold with egg whites into the gelatin mixture, blending thoroughly. Spoon into a 6 or 7-cup ring mold. Chill until firm. To serve, unmold and decorate with a holly wreath made of gumdrops and cinnamon candies. Makes 10 servings.

RASPBERRY PARFAIT

Into parfait glasses, put alternate layers of vanilla or eggnog ice cream and thawed frozen raspberries, starting with ice cream and ending with berries. Top each parfait with a dollop of whipped cream and, if desired, a green maraschino cherry.

FOODARAMA FREEZER TIP: The really smart hostess makes her parfaits a day ahead and stores them in the Foodarama. For this procedure, do not put the last layer of raspberries on the ice cream. About an hour before serving time, remove the parfaits from the freezing compartment; top each parfait with raspberries and whipped cream, then return them to the Fresh Food Compartment of the Foodarama until time to serve.

COCKTAIL PARTIES

Rapidly becoming one of our most popular fashions in informal entertaining, the cocktail party is also one of the simplest to give. From the intimate little "come over for cocktails" gathering to the elaborate, full-scaled cocktail party, success depends almost entirely on good planning, well in advance. Once the guests begin to arrive, your only remaining responsibilities are passing the canapes, nudging your spouse when the shy guest's glass is empty, and enjoying yourself and your guests tremendously.

The "little" cocktail party is practically effortless—a few friends are invited in, most often in the late afternoon, pre-dinner hours. The experienced hostess sets a deadline in her invitation—cocktails from "4 to 6," or "5 to 7." Cocktails are served from a tray, around the living-room coffee table, in front of a roaring fire or on the patio. A nearby sideboard or table holds all the appurtenances for a self-service bar: cocktail napkins; 6 to 8-ounce glasses (better than too-tall glasses in which drinks may get warm and diluted); filled ice bucket (replenished from your well-stocked Foodarama); bar spoon; jigger; mixers of soda, ginger ale and water; a bowl of lemon twists; a bottle each of Bourbon and Scotch; at least one non-alcoholic drink, plus the tray of cocktail glasses and shaker or pitcher of Martinis (or Manhattans). Guests are requested to be their own bartenders or the man of the house takes over the job. Cocktails may be made three or four hours in advance and stored in the Fresh Food Compartment of your Foodarama. Add a few ice cubes just before serving.

The hostess passes the canape trays frequently, along with tiny cocktail napkins, and then places the trays where guests may conveniently serve themselves.

At the large cocktail party, the self-service bar may be used or a few friends of the host might take turns pinch-hitting as bartenders so the host is left free to circulate among his guests. A buffet table is set with candles and flowers, serving forks and spoons, small napkins, small plates and constantly replenished trays and platters of canapes and dips.

HORNS O'PLENTY
(see pic. below)

Prepare a recipe for Pastry (see page 28). Cut heavy-duty aluminum foil into 4-inch squares; roll into horn shapes.

Roll out the pastry 1/8 inch thick; cut into 3-inch squares. Roll each square around a foil horn. Pinch loose edges of dough to seal; place, sealed edge down, on a cooky sheet. Bake in a hot oven, 425°, 10 minutes or until brown. Cool; carefully remove foil. Just before serving, fill the pastry horns with Shrimp Dip (see recipe on page 124). Makes 12 to 15 horns.

Sardine Strips
(see pic. below)

Sprinkle small sardines with a little lemon juice; let stand 10 minutes. Brush strips of toast with melted butter. Place 1 or 2 sardines on each strip. Top with little pieces of partially fried bacon. Place in broiler 4 inches from heat, 5 minutes, or until bacon is crisp and sardines are hot.

SALAMI CORNUCOPIAS

Make cornucopias of thinly sliced salami or bologna and secure them with wooden picks. Fill with well-seasoned cottage cheese mixed with chopped green or ripe olives. Garnish with minced parsley or chives, and paprika.

SHRIMP DIP
(see pic., page 123)

10 large cooked shrimp
1/4 cup mayonnaise
1 tsp. lemon juice
1 tsp. grated onion

1/2 tsp. Worcestershire sauce
Dash pepper
1/4 tsp. salt
Cream

Peel and devein shrimp. Mash to a puree in a food mill or blender. Add next 6 ingredients and enough cream to make mixture spread easily. Serve as a dip with crackers or potato chips or in Horns O'Plenty (see recipe on page 123). Makes about 1 cup.

AVOCADO DIP

2 ripe avocados
1 cup sour cream

1/4 tsp. salt
2 Tbsp. prepared horseradish
1/4 cup grated onion

Cut avocados in halves. Remove seeds and peel. Mash avocados with a wooden spoon; beat until smooth. Stir in remaining ingredients. Makes about 2 cups.

CHEESE DIP

Put *8 oz. cream cheese* and *2 oz. blue cheese* in a small bowl. Mash with a fork. Add *1 Tbsp. lemon juice, 1 tsp. Worcestershire sauce, 1 Tbsp. mayonnaise* and *1/4 cup light cream.* Beat until smooth. Makes about 1½ cups.

CORNED BEEF MINCE

Combine *2 cups minced, canned corned beef, 1/3 cup mayonnaise, 1/3 cup minced celery, 2 Tbsp. pickle relish, 1 Tbsp. grated onion* and *1 Tbsp. prepared horseradish.* Serve as a dip. Makes 2 cups.

CURRIED OLIVES

Pour the liquid from *1 can (9 oz.) ripe olives* into a small saucepan. Add *1/2 tsp. curry powder* and *1 tsp. Worcestershire sauce.* Heat mixture to boiling; pour over olives. Cover and let stand 1 day before serving.

DILLED GARLIC OLIVES

Pour the liquid from *1 jar (9¾ oz.) green olives* into a small saucepan. Add *1/4 tsp. Tabasco sauce, a peeled clove of garlic* and *1/4 tsp. dill seeds.* Heat mixture to boiling. Pour over olives in the jar. Replace cover. Store in the Fresh Food Compartment of your Foodarama 3 or 4 days before serving.

INDEX

125

INDEX

INDEX

INDEX